PERSONS WHO ARE POEMS FROM HIGH SCHOOL

ANNOTATED REMINISCENCES OF FRIENDSHIP AND PREJUDICE

Jeff Nisker MD PhD

IGUANA

Publisher: Cheryl Hawley
Front cover design: Jonathan Relph

ISBN 978-1-77180-750-0 (paperback)
ISBN 978-1-77180-757-9 (hardcover)
ISBN 978-1-77180-749-4 (epub)

This is an original print edition of *Persons Who Are Poems from High School*.

To Mr. Perkins

Table of Contents

About the Author

Jeff Nisker, MD, PhD, is a physician and playwright, scientist and educator, bioethicist and writer. His works immerse audiences and readers in the inequities of new scientific capacities, and the erosion of access to the optimum healthcare that once defined Canada. Jeff's plays have been performed throughout Canada and the United States, as well as in the United Kingdom, Australia, and South Africa. Six of Jeff's plays were collected in *From Calcedonies to Orchids: Plays Promoting Humanity in Health Policy.* Jeff was the subject of a "Profile" in the *Canadian Medical Association Journal* in 2020 that the Editors titled "Theatre of Social Justice."

Jeff's numerous research and education awards include Canada's Royal Conservatory of Music "Excellence in Education Award," which "recognizes the efforts of an outstanding educator who embraces the idea that the arts have the capacity to change the world." Jeff has also won Western University's "Scholar Award for Innovation in Research and Education," as well as the Society of Obstetricians and Gynaecologists of Canada's "President Award" for his significant contribution to Women's Health. Jeff has held and co-held Canadian Institutes of Health Research and Health Canada grants to explore public engagement for health policy development through original full-length theatre. Jeff has served on the Editorial Boards of *Journal of Medical Humanities* and *Ars Medica,* and was the International Representative on the Board of the Centre for Literature and Medicine.

Jeff was chosen by the Canadian Broadcasting Corporation as one of the 13 "Best Minds of Our Time" in the program's inaugural year.

Prelude

The combination of "lockdown"[1] and cancer
Rotated the serrated-steel knob
At the tarnished centre of the scraped gray numbers
Keeping shut my high school locker's
Kick-dented military-green door
Fixed to a row of ten similar kick-dented doors
Standing at attention in a cohort of seventy such rows
In the basement of our century-old high school

The Boys Locker Room's asbestos-foamed ceiling
Striped with narrow hot water pipes
Invited students like me to surreptitiously
Snatch the lock off a neighbour's open locker
And jump up and dunk the lock
On the hot water pipe above his locker
Then jump up again to lock it
Before making an innocent exit

When one is locked away one tries to escape
And the escape for me has been through unlocking
These sublimated high school stories
That without "lockdown" would have remained locked away

---

[1] "Lockdown" was the term for the government-mandated closures during the COVID pandemic.

Preventing reminiscence of persons who sculpted my existence
Persons I wish were still with me in more than reminiscence
Persons never truly locked away for they've influenced my every decision
In the half-century since I last kicked my locker's door

Introduction

In *Persons Who Are Poems From High School,* linked narratives explore today's ethics problems; problems that probably existed but seemed less prominent when Pierre Elliot was Prime Minister.[2] At that time I was ignited by high school, excited by orchestra, sports, girls, and even the wisdom of some of my teachers, but ignorant of many ethics problems regarding women. I include as an ethics problem lack of access to oral contraception, sentencing pregnancy to many high school girls[3] because of misogynistic prejudices that still exist today. Such as physicians' private perspectives,[4] parents' religious convictions, pharmacists' corporate restrictions, and teenagers' financial conditions.[5] Another problem was discrimination against immigrants,[6] which may be even more flagrant today,[7] as

---

[2] Pierre Elliott Trudeau was Canada's Prime Minister in my later years of high school.

[3] See Chapter 3 "Frank and Suzy."

[4] Including sexual intercourse should be reserved for marriage, and that the birth control pill promoted promiscuity.

[5] Contraception only became publicly funded in our province in February 2024 "OHIP covers birth control for women under 25 years old as long as they aren't covered by a private plan."

[6] See Chapter 5 "Friendly Salvatore."

[7] See "COVID Aggression Condemns a Muslim Family Near Our Medical School" *In* Nisker, *Love and Injustice in Medicine,* Iguana Books, 2022.

discrimination in my high school was tempered because most of us were immigrants or their children. Any blatant discrimination came from whiter-skinned male teachers,[8] though I seemed exempt for some reason, and indeed enjoyed going to high school.[9]

I eagerly woke up each morning of high school, at least after the repeated door knocks of Mark,[10] then rushed out that door with brushed teeth and my briefcase,[11] and a buttered slice of white Wonder Bread. My mother had encouraged it into my hand as if it was a baton in a 400-metre relay; however, you don't eat the baton in a relay, and the Wonder Bread was gone before we hit the curb. On our mile and half slog to high school, uphill against the wind both ways in winter, Mark and I always had much to discuss, such as the important game coming up. Which it seemed there always was in one sport or another, and we even looked forward to the sadistic practices, but of course couldn't admit this even to each other.

We were interested in the girls in our "Collegiate," and as our high school years progressed, the women they had magically blossomed, though neither of us ever seemed to be "going steady." We were interested in each other's plans for the future, especially for the upcoming Saturday night, and we would often go down to Yorkville to hear folk music float from "The Riverboat."[12] My high school years were truly privileged, unlike my first generation Italian

---

(Migneault J. Northern Ontario man nearly killed in road rage incident hopes driver who was charged gets help he needs. CBC News, Jan 3, 2025. https://www.cbc.ca/news/canada/sudbury/road-rage-temiskaming-shores-1.7421969)

[8] See Chapter 5 "Friendly Salvatore."

[9] Of course enjoying high school is surprising to the many of you who found high school intolerable.

[10] See Chapter 9 "High School Best Friend Mark."

[11] Backpacks were not in vogue yet except for hikes and canoe trips.

[12] There were many other coffee houses in Yorkville when we were in high school, including the "Mynah Bird," "Night Owl," and "Gaslight." Music drifted through their open doors, so you never needed a ticket to hear Joni Mitchell or Gord Lightfoot. Alas, these coffee houses have been converted into expensive boutique shopping.

friends,[13] who laboured weekends with their fathers, not to mention every day in the summers. While I only had a job in the summers, because my father insisted I focus on school.[14]

These high school stories have become more urgent since I saw the French operatic film "The Umbrellas of Cherbourg"[15] on television, a film I saw in high school with my non-girlfriend Gail.[16] A young Catherine Deneuve sings the lead role in an intimate rather than operatic voice. I would never have thought that an opera could transport my heart back so powerfully to the warmth of my high school years, more than a half-century since graduation. However, the film also imbued the cold intimacies of a late-sixties teen, still struggling with the assassinations of President Kennedy and Dr. King, while witnessing "the horrors"[17] of the Vietnam War on TV.

The stories in *Persons Who Are Poems From High School* are far from being inclusive, and the selection of persons and events are far from privileging their importance. My explanation for why I needed "lockdown" to unlock these stories is that I had the time, as I was "Confined to the COVID Sidelines"[18] by my colleagues, who feared my chemo-subimmunity would cause COVID to claim me.

---

[13] See Chapter 5 "Friendly Salvatore."

[14] See "You Must Go to Medical School or Hitler Will Have Won" *In* Nisker, *Love and Injustice in Medicine*, Iguana Books, 2022.

[15] *The Umbrellas of Cherbourg* (1964), written and directed by Jacques Demy, is technically an opera as it has no spoken words. This film echoes in many World War II films, as Cherbourg was an important deep-water port for the Allies "D Day" landings that would eventually liberate Europe from the Nazis.

[16] Gail and I saw *The Umbrellas of Cherbourg* at the Bayview Theatre when it was a cinema specializing in "foreign" films. It was soon converted into the Bayview Playhouse, where Gail and I saw "Jacques Brel is Alive and Well and Living in Paris" by Bertolt Brecht (See Chapter 15 "The Girl Everyone Thought I Would Marry").

[17] "The horrors" as they were used by Marlon Brando portraying Colonel Kurtz in Francis Ford Coppola's 1979 Oscar-winning film on the Vietnam War, *Apocalypse Now*. The film is based on Joseph Conrad's 1899 novel, *Heart of Darkness*, set in the Belgian Congo.

[18] Nisker, *Confined to the COVID Sidelines: New and Selected Verses*, Iguana Books, 2023.

Chapter 1

Miss Kingsbury Teaches

Comprehension

Miss Kingsbury was a newly minted teacher
Who started at our "Collegiate" with us
Though she looked too young to be a teacher
And was often mistaken for a pretty Senior
Miss Kingsbury taught us Grade 9 English
But more important was our home room teacher
Meaning we started each morning giving her our attention
While we stood at attention for "O Canada"[19]

When Miss Kingsbury returned my first English exam
It was ridden with red question marks
On every long page of the foolscap[20]
And she asked me to speak with her after class
As the end-of-class bell's drilling ended

---

[19] "O Canada" blared from a toaster-size "loudspeaker" in the corner of the ceiling near the front door. (In our high school all classrooms had a front door exit and back door to enter.)

[20] "Foolscap," believe it or not, was what the long pages of lined paper with wide spaces between lines was called.

Miss Kingsbury requested I come up to her desk
Which of course I more than eagerly did
Because of course I had more than a major crush on her

Miss Kingsbury smiled at me and gently said
"Jeff I had to pass you on your English exam
Because you've basically memorized all of *Twelfth Night* [21]
But you don't understand the play or my questions for that matter"
I replied "That's because I can't read with comprehension"
As if I was proud of this formerly irrelevant fact
And proud of Miss Kingsbury for ascertaining this
After just three months of trying to teach me

The mantle of "Can't read with comprehension"
Had been bestowed on me two years previously
By the Standard Grade 7 Aptitude Tests
That we endured to "stream"[22] us for our future
Fortunately I scored high in Math
Or I would have been banished to the district's tech school
Many kilometres further away
To learn a trade in order to be useful

Miss Kingsbury assured me she would remedy my reading
And handed me *To Kill a Mockingbird* [23]
Which I reluctantly put in my briefcase [24]
After promising I would start reading it that evening

---

[21] *Twelfth Night* by William Shakespeare is supposed to be a comedy, but we unanimously considered it silly rather than humourous, and thus a curricular tragedy.

[22] "Streaming" seemed awkward then, and in retrospect offensive, as it promoted elitism.

[23] A novel by Harper Lee (1960). The movie version (1962), directed by Robert Mulligan, and starring Gregory Peck as Atticus Finch, won three Academy Awards.

[24] When I was in high school backpacks were only used on hikes and canoe trips.

However I silently added the caveat
"That is, if there happened to be time
After basketball and supper and homework
And, of course, the Late Night Film on Channel 7"[25]

I actually did plan to read a bit after the film
Having been an insomniac since birth[26]
But the novel was so incredibly compelling
I had it all read before dawn
When I handed Miss Kingsbury her book back
I asked if I might borrow it again for the weekend
Miss Kingsbury smiled a knowing smile
And handed *To Kill a Mockingbird* back to me

I had never read a real novel before
But loved the comic book versions in *Classics Illustrated*[27]
Including *Les Misérables*[28] and *Mutiny on the Bounty*[29]
And *Moby Dick*[30] and *Don Quixote*[31]
I wanted to confess to Miss Kingsbury
That I would love to be able to read real novels
Like I sometimes saw girls carrying
But being a guy I couldn't admit this of course

So I immersed myself in *To Kill a Mockingbird*
Reading it over and over till the weekend was over
And before that wondrous weekend had to finish

---

[25] Curtains went up on WKBW Buffalo's "Late Night Film" at 11:25 p.m.
[26] According to my mother.
[27] *Classics Illustrated* is a series of thicker comic books, edited by Albert Kanter, published by Gilberton Co.
[28] *Les Misérables* (1862) by Victor Hugo.
[29] *Mutiny on the Bounty* (1932) by Charles Nordhoff and James Norman Hall.
[30] *Moby Dick* (1851) by Herman Melville.
[31] *Don Quixote* (1605) by Miguel de Cervantes.

I was sure I wanted to be Atticus Finch[32]
I wanted to have his commitment to justice
His kindness and respect for all persons
His quiet competence and modesty[33]
His unlimited patience and restraint[34]

When I handed Miss Kingsbury her book back
She asked if I wanted to discuss it with her after school
Of course I said "Yes" albeit hesitantly
Because I would be punished with "the steps"[35] for late for practice
However Atticus was just too important to me
As was the opportunity to be alone with Miss Kingsbury
But our discussion of the injustices in *To Kill a Mockingbird*
Almost made me forget I was with Miss Kingsbury

Miss Kingsbury gave me another novel
Then another novel and then another
And after devouring them all albeit just once
I developed a lifelong love of literature
A love that still has me devouring novels
Perhaps not as rapidly as I did in high school
As there's no opportunity to return them to Miss Kingsbury
Although I'll always think of her fondly

---

[32] Atticus Finch is a lawyer asked to defend an innocent black man amidst 1930s American South racism. I wanted to be a lawyer like Atticus Finch, advocating for justice. I wanted to be a father like Atticus Finch, teaching his children through his example as well as words.

[33] Atticus's children had no idea that their father was "the best shot in the county" until the sheriff asked Atticus for help with a dangerous rabid dog.

[34] Such as when a disgruntled white man, fuelled by racist hate and alcohol, spit in Atticus's face for defending a black man. Atticus just wiped the spit off with a handkerchief, rather than punching the lights out of the spitter.

[35] "The steps" punishment was having to run four long flights of steps ten times.

Chapter 2

Friday Night Dances

On Friday nights once a month
Our "Vice" permitted us gym dances
Sponsored by the Students Council
Or Athletic Association or Drama Club
With proceeds from the dollar-each tickets
Going to the sponsoring organization
Except in the fall when self-interest dissolved
And all was donated to the United Appeal[36]

The tickets were sold at a long table
Dragged from the cafeteria down to the gym's foyer
And on that table stood a tall glass jar
We hoped would soon overflow with dollars[37]
And from that table's welcoming edge
Gold Bristol board was masking tape suspended
Modestly masking the pastel-coloured underwear
The miniskirted ticket-sellers liked to wear

The gold Bristol board declared in large letters

---

[36] Known today in Canada as the United Way.
[37] Dollars in Canada were inky paper when I was in high school. "Loonies" would not appear for twenty years.

Drawn with thick red and blue[38] Magic Markers
The recipient of the glass jar's dollars
For that particular Friday Night Dance
As well as an encouraging reminder
To put the next Friday Night Dance on your calendar
And to bring more food cans for our bank
To be accessed by families of our school's less fortunate students

In addition we set up a snack table
Sprawling with chocolate bars and cellophaned muffins
And pop cans of various brands
To raise funds for international causes
Of course no alcohol was on the table
And rarely did anyone sneak a "mickey" in
As we were having too much fun flat-out dancing
To tempt gin as a reason for being kicked out

The recipient of the funds was unimportant to us
We showed up because we just loved dancing
Especially to the Rolling Stones
My favourite band then and now
We demanded the DJ spin "Satisfaction"
And "Get Off of My Cloud" and "Paint it Black"
Then blast them over and over again
We just couldn't get enough of them[39]

When we got exhausted we requested a clinger
Such as the Stones's "As Tears Go By"[40]

---

[38] Red, blue and gold were our school colours. Indeed, our school song began with "Colours red and blue and gold."

[39] The songs of The Stones formed much of the playlist of our physician rock band Bold Fingers. I would lobby my bandmates to play "Brown Sugar" and other songs with long sax solos.

[40] Intimately recorded by Marianne Faithfull, Mick Jagger's girlfriend at the time.

And if there was chemistry in the clinger
We lobbied for "Time is on My Side"
Being late-60s teenagers endowed us with the gift
Of history's most exquisite music
Not only at our Friday Night Dances
But on the transistor radios to which we were affixed

Hundreds of students would come to our Friday Night Dances
As well as a few teachers to be our "monitors"
Hopefully one of them would be Mr. Perkins[41]
Who would never slip his clipboard between clingers
Unlike other teachers who too often did
Or like Mrs. Rose[42] dislodge us with her yardstick
And if we were clinging too hard to pry us apart
She would smack a shoulder with it

Bookending the double doors to the gym
Two stoic gunless policemen[43] stood at attention
Stone-faced and silent keeping an eye on the "lineup"
To the door of the Boys Bathroom
In which we were scraping off the mud
Accrued to our shoes from our shortcut
And our shoes had to be leather-soled "Italians"[44]
To slide smooth on our gym's wood floor[45]

Above our "Italians" white socks were compulsory
Prominently displayed below our black dress pants

---

[41] See Chapter 4 "Favourite Teacher Mr. Perkins."
[42] See Chapter 12 "Wild Mrs. Rose."
[43] I don't remember many policewomen on the Toronto Police Force when I was in high school.
[44] The object of desire for impeached President Richard Nixon in Oliver Stone's 1995 film *Nixon*.
[45] The smooth leather soles of my Italians were the antithesis of the sticky-rubber soles of my Chuck Taylor basketball shoes (See Chapter 6 "Black Chucks").

That fashion demanded be two inches shorter
Than would be considered appropriate today
In Senior Year "bell-bottoms" appeared
That completely covered our white socks
Not to mention much of our Italian shoes
And soon our bell-bottoms turned denim blue

Our Friday Night Dances were largely undated
So we were free to dance clingers with almost anyone we wished
And fast songs with everyone in frantic chaos
As our mantra was "dance till you drop"
Sometimes we would form two inward-facing lines
And gradually migrate to the top opposite our partner
Before dancing together down the human canyon
Like a languorous river along its bottom

The last dance was the most important
And it always had to be a romantic clinger[46]
That would start with making eye contact[47]
With one's favourite clinger-partner
And we always hoped that the last dance
Would be a total "crotch-soaker"
But that depended on your partner
And if the song was long enough for her

For those of you too young to have attended gym dances
I recommend either film version of *West Side Story*[48]

---

[46] Often by The Letterman, such as "When I Fall in Love" (written by Victor Young and Edward Heyman), or "The Way You Look Tonight" (written Jerome Kern with lyrics by Dorothy Fields).

[47] "Eye contact" as a subtle method of engaging your hoped-for dance partner is demonstrated in the film *Dance with Me* (1998) directed by Randa Haines.

[48] *West Side Story* is a Broadway musical brilliantly composed by Leonard Berstein, with lyrics by Stephen Sondheim, choreography by Jerome Robbins, and book by Arthur Laurents. The 1961 film, directed by Robert

Focusing on the dance scenes in the gym
Rather than the rumble scenes in the street
Though we did have rumbles at our Friday Night Dances
Usually on the street near the gym's foyer entrance
Close enough for participants to have an audience
But far enough to be out of sight of the two policemen

I would sometimes intervene in these skirmishes
With calming words like Tony's in *West Side Story*[49]
However I was careful with my calming
When switchblades were flashing
Or bicycle chains swinging
Or Harleys[50] viciously circling
Always wishing that Salvatore[51] was with me
To have my back in better Italian

Violence was rare at our Friday Night Dances
But machoism was more than prevalent
And often wore a black-leather jacket

Wise and Jerome Robbins, won ten Academy Awards including Best Motion Picture. The more recent film version (2021), directed by Steven Spielberg with screenplay by Tony Kushner, won seven Academy Awards. The more recent version has the advantage of the woman portraying "Maria," Rachel Zegler, doing her own singing, rather than the Marni Nixon "voice-over" like she did for Natalie Wood in the first film version (1961), as well as for Deborah Kerr in the *King and I* (1956), and for Audrey Hepburn in *My Fair Lady* (1964).

[49] "Tony" is the central male character in *West Side Story*, who tries to promote peace between his second generation "American" friends and the first generation "Puerto Ricans" who recently moved into the neighbourhood. The imperative for Tony's persistence for peace lies largely in his love for "Maria," who just arrived from Puerto Rico. As you may have sensed, *West Side Story* is a musical update of Shakespeare's "Romeo and Juliet," and even includes the famous balcony scene, albeit on a rickety iron fire escape.

[50] Harley Davidsons were the powerful motorcycles with high handlebars dominant in high school.

[51] See Chapter 5 "Friendly Salvatore."

And slicked-backed "duck-tail" hair
And when not wearing a black-leather jacket
A pack of "Luckies"[52] was often prominent
Tucked under a very short sleeve of a tight black T-shirt
Even if the T-shirt's wearer didn't smoke

The cigarette pack was the important final touch
To the "Don't mess with me" message
Yet I never perceived anyone in high school as dangerous
Even when a dangerous persona was attempted
Rather I was dismayed by my "well-behaved" friends
Who went out of their way to avoid these guys
Whether or not the leather jacket bore an insignia
Or frequented the curved-chrome back of a Harley

Not everyone came to our Friday Night Dances
Some of the guys were too inhibited
Some of the girls too concerned they'd be "wall flowers"
But these girls had no need to fear
Because some of us "nice guys" made a point of picking
A "wall flower" off the "wall flower wall"
And encourage her to immerse in the chaos
That was our Friday Night Dances

We "nice guys" would even hold a "wall flower"
For one slow dance each albeit loosely
Before returning her reddened back to the safety
Of our gym's cool smooth brick wall
That was the closest to deflowering
That would occur for most of us in high school
Because we feared "making a girl pregnant"
And having to drop out to find employment[53]

---

[52] Lucky Strikes were the macho cigarettes until the "Marlborough Man" came along on his horse.
[53] See Chapter 3 "Frank and Suzy."

The birth control pill had just become available
But none of the girls I knew were on it
Because of fear of its threatened complications
Or fear of being considered promiscuous
Even toward our high school graduation
When some of the girls became "fully sexually active"
Fear of "the pill" made condoms our method
Thus pleasure dissipated in pregnancy-fear

I still love dancing and mourn lack of opportunity
With the exception of an occasional wedding[54]
As I don't go to "Clubs" because I'm not sure "Clubs" want me
Because I'm a senior who doesn't drink much
Though I see "Seniors Clubs" advertised on TV
With grey-hairs dancing to songs from the late 60s
But I don't see me in these TV commercials
Because my image of me dancing is much younger

However dancing still brings joy to my heart
And I sometimes find myself dancing at home
When "The Stones" come on the radio
Even if I have to dance to "The Stones" alone[55]
Or when I see a TV ad for ordering
A "Greatest Hits" CD from our high school years
With songs from our Friday Night Dances
Dances I so miss as I reminisce here

---

[54] The last time I danced was at the wedding of a medical student.
[55] In June 2024, WQLN Public Television aired *Rolling Stones: GRRR Live!*, a "special" featuring songs from the late '60s performed by much older Stones. Yet Mick Jagger danced around the runway as if he still was in his twenties, and looked remarkably similar to how he looked when I was in high school. However, time was not on the side of Keith Richards (paraphrased from "Time is On My Side" by Jaggers and Richards).

Chapter 3

Frank and Suzy

Frank and Suzy were the idyllics
At our Friday Night Dances[56]
Frank was two years ahead of us
And Suzy was in our year but none of my classes
Thankfully as she would have been a relentless distraction
As Suzy was the cutest girl in our high school
As well as one of the friendliest
And yes I had a massive crush on her

Frank was captain of our senior football team
And captain of our senior basketball team
And City Champion in three track distances
And record-setter in the javelin
Suzy was of course a cheerleader
And did backflips after Frank's successes
While the rest of us cheered Frank from the bleachers
Along with many of the teachers

---

[56] See Chapter 2 "Friday Night Dances."

Frank was a double-letter winner
And proudly wore a red-and-blue-and-gold V[57]
On each side pocket of his creamy cardigan
Like you see on athletes in 60s movies[58]
We idolized Frank because of his athletic ability
But even more because of Suzy
They were our high school's acknowledged royalty
Though they modestly tried to be like the rest of us

I also idolized the loving relationship
Frank and Suzy clearly possessed
Always holding hands in the hallways
Where they met up between classes
And on the cement steps of our school's front entrance
Where Suzy sat on Frank's knee after lunch
Leaning into him indicating possession
Leaning into him indicating love

Frank's left arm wrapped around Suzy's shoulders
However his right hand held a cigarette
But at least he was careful to blow the smoke away
From Suzy's adoring adorable face
And I couldn't help but appreciate
The love Frank displayed in this gesture
Even before it was unanimously accepted
That cigarettes were clearly causative of cancer[59]

---

[57] Our school song started with "Colours red and blue and gold."

[58] One of the pop groups in the late-60s was called "The Lettermen."

[59] Although cigarettes had been linked to lung cancer before I started high school (Doll R., Hill A. B. 1950. Smoking and carcinoma of the lung: preliminary report. British Medical Journal, 2, 739–748), the enormity of the link was not yet appreciated because of the well-funded denials by "Big Tobacco" (Gannon J, Bach K, Cattaruzza MS, et al. Big tobacco's dirty tricks: Seven key tactics of the tobacco industry. Tob Prev Cessat. 2023 Dec 20;9:39. doi: 10.18332/tpc/176336).

Frank and Suzy dropped out of high school
After Suzy became pregnant
Frank dropped out as soon as they learned
And began working at two jobs
Suzy received the Vice Principal's permission
To continue classes till nearer her due date
When Suzy's once-thin abdomen had become more prominent
Than this future obstetrician could imagine

Eventually Suzy's very pregnant abdomen
Made walking more than challenging
But Suzy confidently waddled the halls
Still smiling at everyone including me
Suzy was the first girl I knew
Who would become pregnant in high school
But she wouldn't be the last as access to "the pill"
Would remain problematic all through high school[60]

The last time I saw Frank I was in Grade 11
And instead of him being on an athletic scholarship
Frank was a flashlight-bearing usher
In the aisles of the Imperial Theatre[61]
I smiled at Frank as he showed my date and I to our seats
And wanted to shake his hand with admiration
And tell him he was my sports inspiration
But I did neither as Frank didn't acknowledge me

---

[60] Even years after I graduated high school, teenage girls who tried to access "the pill" still had great difficulty. Indeed they were referred to as "bad girls" by some physicians, though avoidance of pregnancy was the responsible antithesis of "bad." Eventually teenage pill-seekers became a significant part of our Women's Clinic"

[61] The Imperial Theatre was the largest in Toronto (See Chapter 8 "Rag Doll").

Frank probably didn't even recognize me
As a fellow student at his high school
After all Frank had been a superstar
When I was just beginning to twinkle
But I would never shine like Frank did
No matter how hard I practiced and competed
Largely because of Frank
But even more because of Suzy

I drift back warmly to Frank and Suzy
Whenever I hear Bruce Springsteen's "The River"[62]
The first song that blasts from my car's speakers
Whenever I press the ignition button
Perhaps the reason for the CD's prestigious position
Is that "The River" is a masterpiece
But perhaps a more important reason
Is the reminiscence of Frank and Suzy

---

[62] "The River" (1980), written and performed by Bruce Springsteen and the E Street Band.

Chapter 4

Favourite Teacher Mr. Perkins

I still hear the rhythmic clicks
Of Mr. Perkins's chipped baton
On my music stand insisting togetherness
At early morning Stage Band practices
And regular-hour music classes
And the occasional evening concert
And Mr. Perkins's clicks still beat togetherness
At the centre of my heart

Mr. Perkins's baton was white wooden
And known to splinter even break[63]
When Mr. Perkins became too animated
Trying to prevent the Brass Section's escape
Yet even when splintering Mr. Perkins was pleasant
Whether the student could play their instrument like Marabeth[64]
Or attempted to play but had to fake it
Like too many of the rest of us

---

[63] A half-century later Mr. Perkins told me that he had started using his wife Sally's metal knitting needles.

[64] See Chapter 11 "Marabeth the Best of Us."

Mr. Perkins' pleasantness knew no limits
And extended to the reed squeakers
He squeezed into the Stage Band
So they wouldn't feel excluded
And even extended to the meowing violinists
Who populated his orchestra[65]
Purely for inclusive purposes
Yet few knew they needed to "tune-up"

The stress our orchestra inflicted on Mr. Perkins
Was often beyond enormous
Like when we slaughtered Bach's "Fugue à la Gigue"
Because the Second Violins fugued prematurely
And no matter how panic-animated
Mr. Perkins and his baton became
All the "King's horses and all the King's men"
Couldn't put Johann Sebastian together again[66]

And to make matters much worse
Bach's cacophony occurred
On our annual "Music Night" in our school's amphitheatre
Crammed to the rafters with parents and teachers
Thus for the rest of Senior Year
Members of our orchestra acknowledged each other
With "Bach was just awful"
Or just silently shook their heads

The summer after we graduated
From Mr. Perkins's baton clicks

---

[65] In orchestra practices Mr. Perkins's baton beat on the Concert Master (1st violin) stand.

[66] Paraphrased from "All the King's horses and all the King's men couldn't put Humpty together again," the last line of a nursery rhyme (*Mother Goose Story Book* by William Wallace Denslow 1902).

Marabeth[67] and I worked under his leadership
At a children's summer camp
Mr. Perkins was Head Counsellor
And Director of musical-theatre productions
With Marabeth as his piano accompanist
While I was just a swim instructor

Mr. Perkins's camp name was "King"[68]
And in subsequent years when I would meet him
At younger siblings' music occasions
I would kneel to Neil and greet him as "King"
You see Mr. Perkins will always mean to me
Much more than he possibly can imagine
As he bestowed me with more than he can imagine
And he will always be my "King"[69]

---

[67] See Chapter 11 "Marabeth the Best of Us."

[68] I chose "King" for Mr. Perkins's camp name after he admonished me for calling him "Mr. Perkins." My respect for Mr. Perkins prohibited me from addressing him as "Neil" like everyone else did. A half-century later this respectful prohibition continues, and Mr. Perkins continues to admonish me.

[69] In 2023 Allan (See Chapter 16 "Always Serious Allan"), asked me to come with him to visit Mr. Perkins. However, I couldn't take the time off to go to Toronto, so I asked Allan to call me from Mr. Perkins's home. When Allan put Mr. Perkins on the phone, his compassionate voice sounded exactly the same as when I was last with him more than a half-century before, and after a few minutes Mr. Perkins warmly said, "Jeff, here's Marabeth" (See Chapter 11 "Marabeth the Best of Us"). Allan later told me Mr. Perkins looked exactly the same as when he taught us, except for some grey flecks in his reddish hair, and a few lines on his freckled face. Allan said, "It was as if time stood still for Mr. Perkins," and I responded that there wasn't a better person for whom time should stand still. Allan told me Mr. Perkins and his wife, Sally, still live in the same house where they lived when Mr. Perkins taught us and suggested I come to Toronto so that we can visit them together. I responded, "Absolutely," but knew this would never occur.

Chapter 5

Friendly Salvatore

The high school I was fortunate to attend
Was predominantly first-generation Italians
And I was fortunate to become good friends
With an Italian student named Salvatore
Whose English was often "broken"
But always sewn better than my Italian
Though Italian would become my second language
Rather than French though we were mandated to take it

When I spoke to Salvatore in my fractured Italian
He always smiled and nodded his head
Though I'm not sure he understood much of what I said
Rather Salvatore's smile was because I tried
And because Salvatore was genuinely friendly
More than that he was embracingly warm
And still possessed his "old country" effusiveness
That had emigrated with him on his ship

Salvatore's significant musculature
Spoke of him being older than I was
And perhaps inheriting more muscular genes

And definitely working harder in summers
As Salvatore worked alongside his father
In Toronto's burgeoning construction industry
While I was a swim instructor at a children's camp
A difference that would become significant

Salvatore was in the shop elective class
Being "streamed" toward a tech college or no college
While I was in the music elective class
Being "streamed" toward university[70]
Indeed the classrooms in each academic subject
Be it English or science or math
Were inhabited on the basis of this one elective
Which severely limited friendships

However Salvatore played guard beside me
On our high school's Junior basketball team
And he was better than me in basketball among other things
Having played for years in church leagues
And his well-past-puberty presence
Was of strong support to his skinny guard-mate
Who was fast but would never possess
Salvatore's massive strength

Salvatore could be cumbersome with his adult body
That being new to him was hard to control
Such as when he tripped over the foul line[71]
And slid headfirst into the gym's brick wall

---

[70] Both elective-based class composition and "streaming" seemed awkward when I was in high school, and in retrospect offensive, as both promoted difference even elitism.

[71] Tripping over the foul line is an inside joke in basketball, as the foul line is embedded beneath layers of clear smooth lacquer. I think of Salvatore today while I'm running when I see shadows cast on the street by power lines.

Then after a moment of anguish for his teammates
Salvatore bolted up seeming surprised
That we were the slightest bit concerned for him
And said "What's da matta you guys"

Another of Salvatore's basketball incidents occurred
When we played the new "tech school" in our district[72]
That was to be fed by subsequently anointed
"Academic high schools" including ours
During a timeout in that tough game
Salvatore and I sat on our bench to catch our breath
Just as an empty pop can hit his head
Though it was possibly aimed at my head

We knew we were in a rough environment
And the heads of our teammates who "sat the bench"
Were covered with programs to shield paper spitballs
But a pop can was beyond reason
Salvatore who only "sat the bench" during timeouts
Was not used to his head being hit by refuse
So he bolted up and yelled at the crowd
 "Don't throw cans at me I'm Italian like you"

Though kind-hearted Salvatore meant no offense
To his teammates not of Italian origin
He expected a certain degree of tolerance
From his *paysanos*[73] packed in the stands
However our coach didn't see it that way
And after screaming at Salvatore something about "team"
Planted Salvatore on the bench for the rest of the game
Where he became a target for trash again

---

[72] George Harvey.
[73] An Italian expression for persons who had come from the same country.

Another of Salvatore's sports incidents
Occurred in our high school's swimming pool
In which students of the different "streams"
Flowed together into one deep pond
Phys Ed was exclusively "Boys" or "Girls"
A restriction most significant when Phys Ed was swimming
Once a week in our old school's new pool
Because "Boys" had to swim nude[74]

The Phys Ed teacher who taught "Boys Swimming"
Seemed not to like his students for some reason
Especially his Italian students
And Salvatore was his favourite target
This "teacher" displayed his sadistic side
When he made each of us jump off the diving board
And try to swim 25 yards to the pool's distant end
Whether or not the student could swim

The teacher asked for a volunteer to go first
So this summer camp "Bronze Medallion"[75] volunteered
Dove off the board and freestyled[76] the 25 yards
Then did a vertical push-up to stand on the deck
However my punishment for not remembering
"Never volunteer" was to stand shivering
While the few other students who knew how to swim
Jumped off the board and did their naked length

As I shivered I observed non-swimmers

---

[74] Nude swimming for "Boys" was supposedly essential for reasons both hygienic and practical, as the elastic in our bathing suits was thought to clog the pool's filters. However, the girls did not swim nude even though their bathing suits had more elastic material, and some even had foam cups (or so I'm told).

[75] The Bronze Medallion is the Royal Life Saving Society of Canada qualification to be a lifeguard.

[76] Freestyle (also called "front crawl") is the fastest swim stroke.

Trembling in the line behind the diving board
Trembling before their skin was even wet
Trembling because of fear of drowning
And one of the tremblers was Salvatore
So I quickly walked back to the diving board end
And stood beside my trembling friend
Who quickly clutched my upper left arm

And with his well-passed-puberty low voice
Now terrified an octave higher
Half-squeaked half-whispered
"Nisker promise you won't let me drown"
I promised then we watched more students
Slowly swim their naked length
Usually dog-paddling but sometimes sort of bobbing
While Salvatore's place in line was shrinking

When Salvatore was next in line
Mark[77] performed a painful belly flop
And was struggling to get out at the side of the pool
But our "teacher" kept stepping on his fingers
It was Salvatore's turn and he clutched my arm harder
Refusing to go near the diving board's ladder
While our sadistic "teacher" berated him with
"Get on the board and jump or you're going to flunk"

Salvatore climbed up on the diving board
Worriedly walked to its tip and stared at me
Then jumped and sunk like a boulder
So as promised I jumped in after him
And tried to grasp his well-greased hair
While avoiding his bicycling knees
Until I finally purchased a clutch of head curls

---

[77] See Chapter 9 "High School Best Friend Mark."

And frog-kicked us up to the surface

Salvatore gasped for air as I rolled him on his back
And scissor-kicked us to the left side of the pool
Where Salvatore grasped at the slippery white rim tiles
With all he had in a state of panic
All the while I kept reassuring
"Don't worry I've got you Salvatore"
And "I'm not going to let go of you Salvatore"
And "Everything will be all right Salvatore"

Once Salvatore was a bit calmer
And I could take my eyes off of his
I glared daggers at our Phys Ed "teacher"
But was too much of a coward to call him out
Though I should have for what he did to Salvatore
I was sure he would do again in perpetuity
Until someone with more guts than me called him out
Or some poor student drowned

One afternoon basketball practice was cancelled
And Salvatore asked me to go home with him
To help him with a math assignment
And of course it was my pleasure to do so
Salvatore lived just a few blocks from school
In what had become a first generation Italian neighbourhood
Filling the vacuum induced by the moving north
Of its former Ukrainian-Jewish residents

I knew this neighbourhood well
As my maternal grandparents had lived here
After their emigration from a village near Kyiv
And in fact my mother grew up here
And I also lived here until I was two-and-a-half
When my brother was born and we needed more indoor footage

This was before all the neighbourhood's front yard footage
Was converted to vegetable gardens and grape trellises

My grandfather had backyard trellises
Just a few blocks west of where Salvatore lived
And I was washed in reminiscence of his huge wine barrels
In which I stomped grapes to make his strong wine
Salvatore told me his parents also made wine
But I didn't ask him if he stomped the grapes
Salvatore's neighbourhood was vivid and warm
Compared to where I lived in high school with manicured lawns

For our high school's 100th anniversary
A friend on our basketball team a half-century previously
Called trying to convince me into playing
Against our high school's current Senior team
Of course Salvatore had been on our long-ago team
And I would have driven to Toronto to play with him again
But his name wasn't on the list of players
Nor on the list of registrants for the reunion

However this invitation to "The 100th"
Brought Salvatore firmly to my current consciousness
Along with other persons who are poems in this book
And indeed prompted me to write this book
In which I reminisce persons who made me a better person
Persons like Mrs. Rose[78] and Mr. Perkins[79]
Persons like Mark,[80] Sid,[81] Paul,[82] and Saul[83]
And perhaps most of all Salvatore

---

[78] See Chapter 12 "Wild Mrs. Rose."
[79] See Chapter 4 "Favourite Teacher Mr. Perkins."
[80] See Chapter 9 "High School Best Friend Mark."
[81] See Chapter 17 "Quiet Sid."
[82] See Chapter 14 "Solid Paul."
[83] See Chapter 24 "Tall Saul."

Chapter 6

Black Chucks

Salvatore's basketball shoes were white
Like those on every guy of every team we played
As black basketball shoes were considered uncool
Through all my high school days
Basketball shoes were still canvas
Though the epidemic of leather was imminent
That would sentence basketball shoes to expensive
Though leather never augmented performance

When I started playing in grade nine
I wore my father's ancient black PF Flyers
That had graced the hardwood long ago
When my father played "semi-pro"
They were black high-tops[84] that had no tread left
So my butt often "travelled"[85] across the floor

---

[84] All basketball shoes in high school were "high-tops," thought to prevent ankle injury.
[85] "Travelling" was whistled by the ref for taking extra steps or sliding your feet or other piece of your anatomy.

Yet in deference to my father's lauded days[86]
I wanted to stay with black high-tops

So I called around[87] and found a pair of
Black Converse All Stars in size 10
The Chuck Taylor model[88] easily identifiable
By the large blue stars on your ankles
"Black Chucks" are known best today
Because of their prominence in films
Such as *Hoosiers*[89] set in 1951
In which all Hickory Huskers wore black Chucks

However by the time I was in high school
White Chucks had become dominant on professional courts
And thus dominant on high school courts
Relegating the black colour of my Chucks to anachronistic
Indeed in the first game of my first high school season
Each time I dribbled up Runnymede's claustrophobic court[90]
The   crowd   taunted   "Black   Chucks   Black   Chucks"
With a rhyming profanity often added

The crowd's disapproval of my black Chucks continued
Through every basketball game in high school
Albeit disapproval of a new pair of black Chucks each season
With the reason for the abuse remaining unclear

---

[86] I was often reminded by older referees when they saw my name in the lineup that my father had been a great player.

[87] There was no "online" when I was in high school.

[88] Chuck Taylor high-tops are now everyday fashion footwear for teen girls, although more likely seen in lime green or pink, or an even mixture of fluorescent colours.

[89] The 1986 film *Hoosiers* was directed by David Anspaugh, and starred Gene Hackman as "Coach Norman Dale." Coincidentally, the colours of the uniforms of the Hickory Huskers were gold with red numbers, identical to our high school's uniforms.

[90] See Chapter 20 "My Favourite Runnymede Cheerleader."

I wore black Chucks on the court through University
Until Nike took over
And Nike wanted you to purchase
Their more expensive Air Jordan leathers[91]

Chuck Taylors did have a downside
Whether they were black or white or canvas or leather
The double-edged sword of real-rubber soles
That gave you great traction but made your shoes smell putrid
Indeed the lockers of Chuck Taylor wearers
Whether high-top or low-top acolytes
Were easily identifiable by their foul smell
Even when your locker was shut tight

Though the names on the doors of athletic-shoe stores
Changed over the years before Sport Chek took over
I consistently asked the person behind the counter
If their store had "black Chucks" in stock
My query was greeted by raised eyebrows
And often "What's a black Chuck?"
Or sometimes just "What's a Chuck"?
Or sometimes just silence

But a few years ago a pleasant woman
In a downtown London athletic-shoe store
Replied to my lack Chucks ask with a smile
"We don't have black Chucks but we have dark-blue Chucks"
She smiled again and continued
"We also have pink Chucks and lime-green Chucks
And mauve Chucks and multi-coloured Chucks
I'll see what sizes we have in stock."

---

[91] Air Jordans are recognizable by their insignia of a tall slender man dunking a basketball with his legs spread wide. In 2023, a film-tribute to the manufacture of Air Jordans was released titled *Air*, directed by Ben Affleck, starring Matt Damon and Ben Affleck.

It was my turn to smile as I replied
"The dark-blue will do thank you
And I sure hope you have them in size 10"
She smiled again and disappeared
Then returned with a box of dark-blue low-top 10s
Low-top was irrelevant as my competitive days had ended
And in fact I actually preferred low-tops
Because they looked and felt cooler on my feet

However for the past thirty years on the court
I haven't worn black Chucks or white Chucks
Or dark-blue Chucks or any other colour Chucks
As I have to stay off the court because of neck problems[92]
But I have to wear white shoes in the OR
And I prefer white Chucks to the white "Clogs"
That had become standard OR footwear
So I bought a new pair of white Chucks every year[93]

My loyalty to wearing Chucks in the OR
May have been based on their stableness and comfort
But more likely the reminiscence of the black Chucks
I wore on the court during my high school years
However I had forgotten about them being called "black Chucks"
Until a recent phone call from a long-ago teammate[94]
Who reminisced our high school basketball days
Including I was the only player in Toronto wearing black Chucks

His reminiscence along with my writing of this story
Inspired me to seek another pair of black Chucks

---

[92] I had developed the degenerative neck arthritis, common among early laparoscopic surgeons.
[93] Or sooner if my white Chucks became too bloody. ·
[94] Allan was a white-Chuck-wearing power forward (See Chapter 16 "Always Serious Allan").

That I wanted to wear as my everyday shoes
Rather than my red New Balance cross-trainers
Or if absolutely necessary black-leather dress shoes
When dress shoes are required at weddings[95]
And I recently almost purchased black Chucks from the net
But another size 10 enthusiast beat me to them

---

[95] I actually prefer wearing dress shoes to weddings so I can slide smoothly across the dance floor, like I did a half-century earlier at our high school's Friday Night Dances (See Chapter 2 "Friday Night Dances") and at our Proms (See Chapter 26 "The Prom").

Chapter 7

Brilliant Erle

Erle was the smartest of us
Always had the highest marks of us
Always generous with his smarts with us
Always modest of his gift with us
Erle lived a block from Gillda[96]
In the northwest corner of our elementary school district
But Erle was a grade behind us before he "accelerated"
So we didn't really know Erle until high school

Erle's acceleration made him the youngest of us
And for a while the smallest of us
Until Erle went through puberty in grade eleven
And grew his body but not to match his brain
Erle sort of adopted me as an older brother
As he only had a much older sister
Who also happened to be a math whiz
And rumour had it as was their father

---

[96] See Chapter 28 "Gillda and Sam."

There was always an aura of happiness
Behind the thick lenses of Erle's black-rimmed glasses
Even when Erle had a violin under his chin
Meowing fiercely in Mr. Perkins's orchestra[97]
Erle was eager in orchestra as in everything
Never feeling superior because of his genius
Nor inferior when immersed in sports
With the more coordinated rest of us

Even when our Phys Ed teachers were tough on Erle
He kept his smile and just tried harder
But Erle's Phys Ed mark lowered his overall average
From astronomical to closer to the rest of us
However a low Phys Ed mark in Senior Year
Would threaten Erle's chances of "First in the Province"
And the enormous scholarships that went with "First"
Which we all thought a ridiculous disadvantage

In second term Phys Ed was gymnastics
And a large part of our mark was graded
On climbing a rope to the gym's rafters
While the rest of us counted the times you made it
But it was hard for Erle to get off the ground
And a zero would nullify his chance for "First"
So we hatched a plot to assist our genius friend
Just as Erle assisted many of us in Physics[98]

Allan[99] distracted our Phys Ed teacher
While I knelt at the rope for Erle to climb on my shoulders
Then I stood up and pushed up his feet
And we repeated this recipe over and over
It wasn't long before our Phys Ed teacher

---

[97] See Chapter 4 "Favourite Teacher Mr. Perkins."
[98] See Chapter 19 "Mr. Kerr's Physics Antics."
[99] See Chapter 16 "Always Serious Allan."

Caught up to our "magic rope trick"[100]
But he thought it "creative teamwork"
So didn't lower Erle's score one bit

Erle sat beside me on "Reach for the Top"[101]
And looked at me worriedly when I forgot
To leave the math questions to him
And my misinterpretation cost us the match
Of course Erle stood first at graduation
But there was a petition for me to be Valedictorian
Because it was thought I would deliver a "more representative"
Not to mention "more humorous" valedictory address

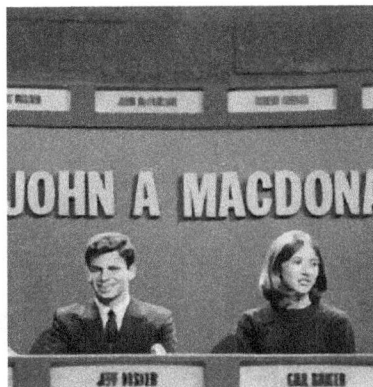

---

[100] Magic rope tricks included the rope stand by itself without the audience seeing the strings being pulled.
[101] See "Reach for the top" pictures below.

However I refused the petition's privilege
As our high school had a long tradition
Of top average being Valedictorian
And Erle thanked me for taking this stand
We became closer after this
A closeness that would soon dissipate at U of T[102]
As Erle's acceptance into prestigious "M P and C"[103]
Put him on a different part of the massive campus

But it was Erle's social life that drifted us apart
Including hanging out at Rochdale College[104] with its marijuana[105]
And this competed with Erle's "M P and C" courses
And consumed his chances of renewing his scholarships
Erle just wasn't yet equipped
To be flying high except in math and physics
And I feel guilty for not being there for him
Though Allan[106] said there was nothing I could have done

Erle finally "got his act together"
And went off hard drugs for a while
And enrolled at a university more lenient for brilliant students
Who had not followed the standard prescription
I lost track of Erle until a recent Zoom call with Gail[107]
On which we went online to search for Erle
Only to find his drug demons became too much for him
And in 2020 he ended his life

---

[102] University of Toronto.
[103] The "Math, Physics and Chemistry" program at U of T was only offered to a few geniuses
[104] "Once Upon a City: Rochdale College and the Hippie Dream," *Toronto Star*. Apr 6, 2017.
[105] There were also "hard drugs" at Rochdale College.
[106] See Chapter 16 "Always Serious Allan."
[107] See Chapter 15 "The Girl Everyone Thought I Would Marry."

I haven't yet recovered from this information
And will always feel guilty for not checking in on him
Because we were close friends in high school
When he considered me his older brother
On the Zoom call Gail and I put our heads together
Like we did when we lost on "Reach for the Top"
Because I forgot to leave the math to Erle
Just like I forgot to keep hugging him after graduation

Chapter 8

Rag Doll

Jenny sat by herself during lunch hour
At a corner of a long cafeteria table
With at least four seats separating her
From the talkative girls not beside her
Jenny never talked during lunch hour
Nor acknowledged others during lunch hour
Nor did Jenny ever eat during lunch hour
Nor have a lunch bag in front of her

Jenny just stared ahead during lunch hour
Her huge blue eyes rivetted on a distant something
While my eyes riveted on Jenny's eyes
Though I tried to deny my eyes their rivet
For I didn't want Jenny to feel uncomfortable
Or more likely me feel uncomfortable
But a half-century later I still feel uncomfortable
As I remain riveted on Jenny

The reason I noticed Jenny sitting alone
My last autumn of high school
Was that Jenny was truly beautiful
Though I doubted Jenny knew she was beautiful
Her subdued blue eyes imbued sadness
As did her persistently-pursed thin lips
And as you have guessed I was smitten by Jenny
Though I tried my hardest to resist

I also couldn't help but notice
The wafer-thin dress Jenny always wore
The same dress every day that autumn
Even after cold weather descended
The threadbare-thinness of Jenny's dress
Lay flat against her near-emaciated body
Transparently revealing the waifness of Jenny
As well as the bra mandated by the school board

On my way out of the cafeteria one November lunch hour
I came upon Jenny being harassed by three guys in my class
In the hall that ran parallel to the cafeteria
Sided by long cork bulletin boards
Decorated with red-thumb-tacked announcements
That none of us ever read
Perhaps because most of the announcements
Were for events that had already happened

Jenny's bullies taunted "Rag Doll Rag Doll"
The chorus of the hit song by The Four Seasons
We heard over and over on 1050 CHUM
Our radio station when we were young
Perhaps worse they were grabbing at the small-brown purse
Jenny usually carried over her left shoulder
But at that moment was swinging as a defensive weapon
So I had to step in to defend Jenny

I inserted my body between the bullies and her
Urging "Come on guys leave her alone"
Amidst the unintended intimate brushes
Of Jenny's windmilling purse down my back
And the urgent venom of Jenny's words
Spitting defiance at her harassers
And pounding pride in my heart
Fueling my desire to protect her

The bullies' taunts didn't have to change direction much
To sling them at me with the addition of "lover"
Becoming "Rag Doll lover Rag Doll lover"
Further awakening my quixotic[108] nature
That would have disregarded the "Rag-Doll-lover" taunts
If they didn't have collateral damage on Jenny
Who moved in tighter behind my body's shield
Seeking protection from the poison projectiles

This "knight in shining armour" wore Jenny's colours
On the handkerchief knotted around my upper left arm
And was rewarded by Jenny's gentle hand
Softly caressing the small of my back
However I felt that I was in trouble
Not from Jenny's harassers as all bullies are cowards
Rather from my autumn-long feelings for Jenny

---

[108] Don Quixote de la Mancha is the self-proclaimed "knight in shining armour" (though his armour is long past shining), who is the central character in the 1605 Spanish novel bearing his name by Miguel de Cervantes. Don Quixote takes on hopeless quests in the name of his Lady Dulcinea, who without his rose-coloured glasses is a "kitchen slut." Don Quixote has many other poetic misinterpretations, such as when he jousts at a windmill that he perceives is a dragon. In 1965, Don Quixote was made into the brilliant Broadway musical, *Man of La Mancha*, music by Mitch Leigh, lyrics by Joe Darion, and book by Dale Wasserman.

And from her possible new feelings for me

When the bell clanged the end of lunch hour
As if it was the bell at the end of a boxing round
Jenny's bullies walked down the hall echoing
"Rag Doll lover Rag Doll lover"
And I felt Jenny's hand pushing firmer
Into the welcoming small of my back
And her warm breath whisper "Thank you"
Before Jenny took hold of my left hand

I reluctantly turned and looked at Jenny
Her now fully-alive eyes sparkling up at me
And I felt myself drowning in the ocean of those eyes
But it must have been a minute before I gasped for breath
I sputtered "No problem" but instead of walking away
Like I knew for certain I should do that day
I said "Let me know if those guys bother you again"
Then stupidly added "Best to just ignore them"

Jenny smiled and said "I thank you again"
Then quickly added "Do you want to go out this weekend?"
I should have just stopped what was happening with "No I can't"
Even though I would have been lying
But for some reason I resisted doing the right thing
As going out with Jenny was definitely not the right thing
Because I didn't want her to think our relationship could go anywhere
As I would be going to university in less than a year

And didn't want to be encumbered with a girlfriend
Let alone a girlfriend still in high school
But heard my voice answer "Sure"
Though I was more sure it was the wrong word
I felt Jenny's hand caress my back firmer
As she urged "Let's go to a movie on Saturday"

My accelerating fumbling feelings for Jenny responded
"Okay but let's go to a matinee"

I thought a matinee would be safer
And obviate the movie being a "Saturday night date"
And the specialness a "Saturday night date" conveyed
Through all my high school days
Jenny said "Pick me up at one and we'll go for a walk
Before heading to the Imperial[109] for their two o'clock"
Then Jenny red-penned her address on my left hand
Smiled at me satisfied and walked away

For two days my internal gaze
Focused intensely on Jenny
Yet I feared seeing her in the cafeteria
Because I feared having to sit beside her
And provoking another round of
"Rag Doll Rag Doll" attacks on her
However I did see her and did sit beside her
To a chorus of "Rag Doll lover Rag Doll lover"

I stood up to put a stop to the harassment
Not of me I couldn't care less
But I did care increasingly about Jenny
And felt awful about how she must feel
Jenny had become my Achilles heel
And my "C'mon guys please" was greeted with laughter
And another chorus of "Rag Doll lover Rag Doll lover"
And I confess it was hard to "Just ignore them"

On Saturday I drove to Jenny's address

---

[109] The Imperial was Canada's largest movie theatre, situated in downtown Toronto across Yonge St. from Eaton's. In Chapter 5 "Frank and Suzy," I recall Frank being an usher in the aisles of the Imperial Theatre after he had to drop out of high school because Suzy was pregnant.

Down a small street I hadn't noticed before
Directly behind the Imperial Theatre
Amidst lightless neon "Exit" signs
Of course I frequented the Imperial with my friends
As it competed with the Odeon for having the best pictures
And was almost next door to "Sam the Record Man"
Where we would explore albums after the film

At Jenny's address there was a parking spot
Almost in front of her squat apartment
I pressed the outdoor button of Jenny's number
And heard her whisper "Why don't you come up"
With a mixture of anticipation and trepidation
I jogged up to the fourth floor
But paused before knocking on Jenny's door
Wondering what was I doing here

Jenny unbolted the door then bolted out the door
Saying breathlessly "Let's go for our walk"
I suggested "Let's go down the stairs first"
And on each landing basked in the bath of her smile
As we exited Jenny hooked my left arm
And excitedly swayed me down the sidewalk
I couldn't bring myself to talk much
Just let my feelings do the speaking

When our walk looped to the Imperial's box office
I bought our tickets then Jenny took my left hand
And pulled me into the Imperial's aging opulence
That began with the doors to its ornate foyer
I felt relief when Jenny declined sharing popcorn
And ordered a large Pepsi instead
That was fizzled into a plastic cup with two straws
So I quickly ordered a small 7-Up

As we entered the enormous theatre[110]
Jenny suggested we sit in the back row
I concurred saying something stupid[111]
Like "We'll see the movie better from back here"
We sort of slid across the folded-up seats
Bumping forward on each no-longer-padded armrest
Till Jenny whispered "These seats okay?"
And I whispered "As long as I can sit beside you"

There were no cup-holders carved in armrests then
So we were accustomed to balancing our drinks
Between an armrest and our proximate leg
Or more frequently between our knees
Jenny did the former I the latter
Before Jenny snuggled in closer
Just as the mandatory pre-feature shorts
Began to clutter the enormous screen

Then Jenny gripped my upper left arm
Forcing me to focus on quelling my emotions
That were so effervescent yet so dread-filled
That I don't remember the feature's title
Rather my memory is tactile with Jenny's body
Snuggling into mine closer and closer
And a few minutes after the feature started
Jenny asked me if I wanted to kiss her

I looked into Jenny's wondrous eyes
But knew for certain I shouldn't kiss her
However I didn't want to offend her
So said "Thank you but let's get to know each other better"

---

[110] Within five years the Imperial would be carved into a "multiplex" of six long narrow theatres and renamed the "Imperial Six." The Odeon would soon be condemned to similar maceration.

[111] As in the song "Something Stupid" by Carson Parks and Gaile Foote.

Jenny's grip on my arm firmed further
As she looked up at me and whispered
"You're obviously a gentleman
And I'm not used to being with a gentleman"

After the film I walked Jenny back to her building
Worrying all the way that she'd ask me into her flat
Then worrying more as we sauntered up the four floors
And walked across the landing to Jenny's door
Jenny unlocked the door and opened it
But quickly pirouetted and put her hand on my chest
"There's someone home so you can't go in
But let's do this again next weekend"

I smiled and gave Jenny a quick hug
And said "I'll see you in the cafeteria on Monday"
Her wondrous eyes smiled but there was sadness there
And I knew for certain I didn't want to go there
But I should have gone there because on Monday
I couldn't find Jenny in the cafeteria
I worried that Jenny was ill
But dreaded her absence meant something different

Yet I waited till Wednesday before I began inquiring
Starting with the girls at Jenny's table
However the girls didn't know where Jenny was
And one of them said "We really don't know Jenny"
So I asked "Do you know someone who does knows Jenny"
But the girls just looked at each other
Then one said "No one really knows Jenny
She just transferred here in September"

That evening I drove to Jenny's address
And pressed the outdoor button of her apartment number
There was no answer but an elderly woman

Was just about to exit the building
So I held the door open for her and quickly entered
Then shouldered open the inside door
And found myself running up to the fourth floor
And pounding hard on Jenny's door

There was no answer so I pounded harder
Until the door across the landing opened a crack
Enough for me to see an elderly woman behind its chain
And I asked her if she knew where Jenny was
The woman whispered "They moved away"
I urged "Do you have a phone number or address"
And heard "That's all that I can say"
Before the door shut and the lock clicked

Next day I entered the Vice's office
And asked his kind receptionist
If she could give me any information on Jenny
But she replied "I'm sorry I can't"
So I asked if I could speak with the Vice Principal
And she pressed a button on the intercom on her desk
Then whispered something I couldn't hear
But after a few minutes the Vice came out of his office

He led me into his sanctum sanctorum
But didn't ask me to sit down
Rather went around his large grey-metal desk
And sat in his enormous tan-leather chair
Then started shuffling papers as if I wasn't there
And worse as if he was irritated
By the disruption of my insolent presence
In the calm of his silent realm

The Vice happened to know who I was
Because of the several committees on which I served

That often required a student meet with him
And too often the student elected was me
I stood silently except for my shuffling feet
Then after more than a few minutes I said
"There's a girl who's not at school
And I'm quite concerned about her"

The Vice raised his eyebrows and after a few seconds
Reluctantly raised his eyes from his papers
And sighed "What's the girl's name?"
And I realized I didn't know Jenny's last name
I replied "Her given name is Jenny
But I'm sorry sir I don't know her family name"
The Vice looked up at me with weary eyes and said
 "Then there's nothing I can do for you"

"But you must be aware of a student who's been absent a week"
He repeated "There's nothing I can do for you"
His edict meant there was nothing he could do for Jenny
Which meant there was nothing I could do for Jenny
This knight in shining armour had been jousted off his stead
And would never possess the same righteousness again
And to this day I regret I didn't push him harder
Because I never saw Jenny again

In the half-century since I last saw Jenny
It has been hard for me to enter the Imperial Theatre
Even if the film was an Oscar winner
Because of the Imperial's proximity to Jenny
In the half-century since I last saw Jenny
Whenever I've been asked to speak at U of T[112]
I decline staying at Eaton's Centre Hotel
Because it's just a few blocks from where Jenny lived

---

[112] University of Toronto.

In the half-century since I last saw Jenny
Whenever I see a paper-thin dress worn in winter
It flashes shivering images of Jenny
And my hope that she is warm somewhere
In the half-century since I last saw Jenny
I've been riveted by large blue eyes of women my age
Because these women may resemble what Jenny looks like today
Because one of these women may be Jenny

In the half-century since I last saw Jenny
I've been burdened by guilty questions
Such as why did Jenny transfer to our high school
Which inflicted more than an hour of subway and streetcar
Had Jenny transferred high schools frequently
Or just once for the months that I knew Jenny
But I didn't really know Jenny
And will always regret that I didn't know Jenny

And finally why after so many years
Have I become so obsessed with Jenny
The answer is I watched a TV documentary
On "Frankie Valli and The Four Seasons"[113]
And when "Rag Doll" was performed
I was swept back a half-century to Jenny
And was wrapped sadly in the song's chorus
As it wrapped me in worry for Jenny

---

[113] A WQLN Public Broadcasting "Special" in 2025 to support programming through the sale of CDs and video discs. I thought of ordering the CD, but reconsidered to avoid painful nostalgia.

Chapter 9

Best Friend Mark

Every high school morning started
With Mark's knock at our front door
At seven-thirty or an hour before
For a morning practice of some sort
I was a religious sleeper-inner
And never considered rousing till Mark's knock
Fortunate sport practices were after classes
And wished this true for music[114]

My mother would let Mark in the door
For him to charm her for the minute I dressed
And brushed my teeth and dashed down the steps
Murmuring "Hi Mark" at my disheveled best
Then quickly step into last season's black "Chucks"[115]
Randomly parked in the vicinity of our front door

---

[114] See Chapter 4 "Favourite Teacher Mr. Perkins."
[115] "Chucks" refers to the "Chuck Taylor" model of Converse basketball shoes (See Chapter 6 "Black Chucks").

As while my mother provided me a slice of white Wonder Bread
Along with a "Be good Jeff" hug[116]

Mark was accustomed to my sleeping in
And subsequent rushing-out ritual
And his importance in knocking me awake
And reminding me to take my briefcase[117]
My best friend didn't mind waiting
Nor diverting his school route from direct
And wouldn't have minded if both were longer
After all that's what best friends are for

Mark and I shared our teenage thoughts
On our mile-and-a-half slog to high school
Across a muddy shortcut in autumn and spring
Uphill against the wind both ways in winter
Mark was the antithesis of self-centered
Rather consistently focused on others
Always interested and compassionate
You couldn't ask for a better best friend

Mark went through puberty before the rest of us
And start shaving and cultivating a moustache
And soon was taller and wider than the rest of us[118]
Thus a solid forward on our Junior basketball team
Mark's density denied being shoved out of "the key"[119]
And promoted his setting "picks"[120] for me
As well as his leading our team in rebounding

---

[116] This front door ritual is also described in the Preface.

[117] Backpacks were not in vogue yet dumping my high school years.

[118] Saul would become a few inches taller than Mark but never as wide (See Chapter 24 "Tall Saul").

[119] "The key" is the keyhole-shaped area under the basket and extending into the court.

[120] The player setting the "pick" stands firmly while his teammate brushes his cover off him.

And "second-opportunity scoring"[121]

Mark was enthusiastic about everything
Even running on our cross-country team
Though his body's larger dimensions
Made long distances harder for him
Mark would have been a superstar in football
But none of our parents would sign the permission form
Because of concern regarding head injuries
Frequently warned of in *The Star*[122]

However Mark's prowess in football was observed
Every weekend in football season in our no-equipment tackle games
The field behind Saul's home[123]
For which we didn't need our parents' permission
Mark was fondly known as "The Boatman"
Because it was impossible to sink him
Even if three of us grasped his legs
And the rest of us jumped on his back

Mark played clarinet right beside me
In Mr. Perkins's Senior Orchestra[124]
And was more serious than me in the orchestra
Especially when we were forced to play Bach
However Mark permitted me the solo *glissando*
To open *Gershwin's* "Rhapsody in Blue"
Because he knew I loved Gershwin
And never minded playing second fiddle

---

[121] Saul would lead our team in these categories by the time we played Senior (See Chapter 24 "Tall Saul").

[122] See Chapter 14 "Solid Paul." Paul forged his father's signature in order to play football, but his father learned about the forgery when Paul was selected an All City All Star by the *Toronto Star*.

[123] Before the field was dug up for the subway's new tunnel (See Chapter 29 "Tall Saul").

[124] See Chapter 4 "Favourite Teacher Mr. Perkins."

In orchestra like in everything
Nothing could sink Mark's joyousness
Until his father's cancer diagnosis
After which I watched both of them wither
On their walks that passed fewer and fewer houses
And required more and more of Mark's support
And Mark knew cancer's too-often conclusion
From visiting my grandmother in my bedroom[125]

Mark's buoyancy kept deflating
And one morning I didn't wake to Mark's knock
Rather to my mother nudging me in tears
"Mark's father died in the night"
I dressed quickly and ran to Mark's house
Where the windows were already shrouded
And thought it would be intrusive to knock
But returned after school and took Mark for a walk

A week after Mark's father's funeral
Mark knocked on our door as usual
And was welcomed by my mother's hug
And her tear-laden "I'm so sorry Mark"
Hearing Mark's knock now prompted
Much quicker wake-up machinations
Before hugging Mark at our front door
And walking to school with him in silence

1967 was Canada's "Centennial"
And one day my mother firmly announced
"Our neighbours are chartering a bus to Expo[126]

---

[125] My grandmother like Mark's father was in her late forties when she died of cancer (See "Princess Margaret" *In* Nisker, *Love and Injustice in Medicine*, Iguana Books, 2022).
[126] "Expo 67" was a World's Fair held in Montreal.

And Jeff you're ordered to be on it"
Of course the last thing I wanted to do
Was to have to sit on a bus for five hours
Packed to the brim with yakking neighbours
But my repeated refusals were ignored

Then it hit me that of course Mark
Would also be ordered on the bus
And we happily boarded that bus together
And planted our bums at the very back
Once the bus was on the 401
Mark opened his grey-vinyl tote bag
And surfaced a beige-paper bag from within
From which peeked a bottle of gin

Mark brought out the gin with a "*voilà*"[127]
As if he was a famous magician
Conjuring a woman from a sworded chest
And the bottle's label read "Tanqueray"
Mark put the bottle back in the paper bag
Then unscrewed the top between his knees
Where the bottle remained hidden unless we were drinking
And it was empty before we reached Montréal

There we fought back the surging urge to vomit
Until the bus stopped at Expo's entrance
Where we flew out the door to puke on the grass
And I don't remember much after that
Except perhaps parents' blurred words
Such as "Of course it serves them right"
And "I'm sure they'll never drink again"
And "Let's just leave them here"

---

[127] *Voilà* is a difficult to translate French word for something like "Take a look at this."

After wiping the vomit off our faces with grass
We picked ourselves up but abruptly collapsed
But it was a glorious sunny day
And we were happy to just lay where we lay
We don't remember much about Expo
Or indeed Montréal in general
As the drinking age was three years lower in Quebec
Thus alcohol appreciatively easy to access

However I do remember that we struck out
Trying to pick up two Quebecois girls
We met beneath the "geodesic dome"
Of the enormous United States Pavilion
Both girls were locals and said they had to go home
But might see us again tomorrow
So Mark gave them his raised-eyebrow smile
And flattered "I sure hope so"

All the way through high school when we "hustled" girls
Mark insisted on doing all the talking
And continuously kept reminding me
"Just keep your mouth shut and try to look pretty"
Though Mark always wanted me to be his "wingman"[128]
He never wanted me to interrupt his script
Because he was worried I might say something stupid
Like "Who is your favourite author"

The next year I had a similar experience with Mark

---

[128] "Wingman" is the term for the pilot of the plane flying beside the lead pilot's plane in combat. In the 2019 film "Midway," directed by Roland Emmerich, the central character Dick Best (portrayed by Ed Skrein), encourages a young pilot who has "lost confidence" by offering to have him as his "wingman," and promises to watch over him. Of course, the young pilot is shot down, and the central character loses confidence.

On our graduation-class trip to Ottawa
To try to meet Pierre Elliott Trudeau
The classiest Prime Minister Canada would ever know
All the girls in our class had a crush on Pierre Elliott
As did many girls across Canada
Displayed in the tidal waves of waving girls
Trying to kiss him wherever he went

The bus driver took us directly to Parliament Hill
Probably because he couldn't stand the shrieking behind him
And the girls flew off the bus to join the hundreds
Waiting where Pierre Elliott was predicted to walk
I had great respect for the girls in our year
Such as Gail[129] and Marabeth[130] and Gillda[131]
That is until they started screaming their guts out
When they saw our graciously-smiling Prime Minister

Neither Mark or I was screaming
Rather we were kissing the grass of Parliament Hill
Trying to hold back the vomit
That could get us into trouble with teachers
We only raised our heads at the apex of the screeches
When all the girls charged forward en masse
Trying to kiss Pierre Elliott
With some of the girls tripping over us

Our Prime Minister waved at the girls
And gracefully accepted cheek kisses
Before the security guards there to protect him
Ripped the too-amorous girls off him
Our Prime Minister wore a red rose
On the lapel of his blue pinstriped suit

---

[129] See Chapter 15 "The Girl Everyone Thought I Would Marry."
[130] See Chapter 11 "Marabeth the Best of Us."
[131] See Chapter 28 "Gillda and Sam."

I'm sure of the rose but not of the suit
As Mark had introduced me to a new bottle of booze

During Senior years Mark and I would drive[132]
Down to Yorkville Saturday evenings
To immerse ourselves in the sea of people
Hovering in the street listening to the music
That overflowed the coffee houses[133]
Like "The Riverboat" and "Owl's Nest"
So there was never a need to buy a ticket
To hear Joni Mitchell or Gordon Lightfoot

And when our parties were short on girls
Party-animal Mark was dispatched to Yorkville
To pick up a few girls just to dance with
And always asked me to be his "wingman"
And as always Mark kept reminding me
"Just keep your mouth shut and try to look pretty"
Thus as always Mark did all the talking
And rarely did we accomplish our mission

Mark was a math wizard of almost Erle's calibre[134]
And would coerce me into entering
Math competitions with him and Erle[135]
Wasting many Saturdays at Waterloo University
Mark's math wizardry became more important to me
When he decided we would become Bridge partners[136]

---

[132] You only needed to be sixteen to achieve your driver's license when we were in high school.
[133] The coffee houses in Yorkville have since been converted to expensive chic boutiques.
[134] See Chapter 7 "Brilliant Erle."
[135] See Chapter 7 "Brilliant Erle," and Chapter 12 "Wild Mrs. Rose."
[136] My grandmother had taught me to play Bridge when I was an overactive child banished to her house on weekends. She taught me a two-handed form of Bridge, and while playing she noticed I had photographic memory. She

To lighten the wallets of the rich kids
Who lived across Bathurst in Forest Hill

Mark's Bridge genius was on his own after high school
Though we both went to U of T[137]
And Mark's passion for collecting "master points"
Soon declared him a "Bridge master"
Mark's math excelled him in "Commerce and Finance"
An undergraduate programme that Mark found easy
And Mark later became a successful accountant
And eventually a finance lawyer

Mark's fewer hours in "C and F"
Compared to mine in Pre Meds and Meds
Couldn't help but drift us apart
After Mark moved in with his new friends near High Park
Where I would visit Mark excessively
Until we drifted further apart when I moved to London
To work with a famous cancer surgeon[138]
And I rarely saw Mark again in person

However we spoke on the phone frequently
And when Zoom came along we used it
Always ending our Zoom calls with a hug

---

told me "Jeff you have been given a gift but it's not for you, it's for the service of others." My grandmother reminded me of "the service of others" throughout my youth, until she died at age 48 of BRCA-gene breast cancer. My mother would suffer the same fate (See the narrative poem "She lived with the Knowledge" (Nisker J, *Ars Medica* 2004, 1(1), 75–80), and the play *Sarah's Daughters* published in *From Calcedonies to Orchids: Plays Promoting Humanity in Health Policy* (Nisker J, Iguana Press 2012). Portions of *Sarah's Daughters* were most recently published in the book *Love and Injustice in Medicine* (Nisker J, Iguana Books 2022)).

[137] University of Toronto.

[138] Dr. Hugh Allen was a world-famous women's cancer surgeon (See "I'm Sorry Vaccine Came Too Late for You Janet" *In* Nisker, *Love and Injustice in Medicine*, Iguana Books, 2022).

Feeling forever our brotherly love
And at my 60th birthday party
One of my sons gave me the great gift
Of "Zooming" Mark into the party
Because it wouldn't have been a party without him

Chapter 10

High School's Darkest Day

Phys Ed had just finished
And as per usual no time to shower
Before pushing out the gym's emergency exit
To "Portable 6" for Geography
As we entered Mr. Fennel's portable
There was our usual jostling and laughing
Before our ritual banging of desks with thick texts
But this day something was amiss

Mr. Fennel's forehead was on his desk
His arms folded behind his lined neck
And his shoulders were heaving with sobs
So of course we got quiet
After a few minutes Mr. Fennel raised his head
And wiped his rimless glasses with a gray handkerchief
And blurry-eyed tried to focus for a minute
Then whispered "The President has been shot"

Mr. Fennel started sobbing again
And blurted "The President was shot in Dallas
While waving to a crowd from his motorcade[139]
And I'm sorry but I can't teach you today"
Silence and sorrow swept over us
As we filed out of Mr. Fennel's portable
And my habitual teenage joyousness
Dissolved in solemn reflection

The wind had been kicked out of me
I was truly having trouble breathing
Certain the second I learned the President had been shot
That if he died my youth would be buried with his[140]
Classes were cancelled for the rest of the afternoon
And Mark[141] and I walked home in silence
Then when alone I turned on the television
In the little "den" off our kitchen
Walter Cronkite[142] was on Channel 4
Giving us more on the President's condition
And after a few minutes Cronkite wiped his glasses
And said "President Kennedy is dead"
Moisture rapidly filled my eyes

---

[139] President Kennedy always insisted his limousine be open-air so he could better engage the waving crowds. This insistence was over the objection of the secret service especially in Dallas, as the ultra-liberal President Kennedy was in greater danger in the American South.

[140] President Kennedy was my high school hero. He was taken to the Emergency Room at Parkland Memorial Hospital. I visit this ER whenever I give a talk in Dallas. I also always kneel on "the grassy knoll" overlooking Elm St. at the site where the president's head exploded. There I occasionally glance over my left shoulder at the Texas Book Depository's fourth floor window, from which Lee Harvey Oswald's rifled had protruded. Conspiracy theories of multiple gunmen in multiple locations abound, as examined in Oliver Stone's Academy Award-winning 1991 film *JFK*.

[141] See Chapter 9 "High School Best Friend Mark."

[142] Walter Cronkite was the CBS Television News anchor when I was in high school. I viewed him most recently on a TV clip in the film *Apollo 13* (1995), directed by Ron Howard, starring Tom Hanks as astronaut Jim Lovell.

And my mother came in and sat beside me
Concerned because I never cried
But my hero had never died[143]

My mother wondered why I was so upset
With the death of another country's leader
And I didn't attempt to explain to her
What the President meant to me
How do you explain his youthful presence
Or the content of his inaugural address
Or his restraint in the "Cuban Missile Crisis"[144]
Or his writing of the Civil Rights Bill[145]

---

[143] Before I graduated high school, the assassination of my other hero Dr. Martin Luther King Jr. would spiral me down to a new level of pessimism. My pessimism would descend further with the shooting of Robert Kennedy, and the killings of four students exactly my age at Kent State University by the Ohio National Guard (*The Fourth of May: Killings and Coverups at Kent State* by William A. Gordon Promtheus Books, 1990). The students at Kent School were protesting Richard Nixon's decision to send American troops into Cambodia. I am transported to Kent State every time I hear Neil Young sing "Four dead in Ohio" in his 1971 "Ohio." Twenty years after high school graduation, I was invited to give a seminar at Kent State, and visited the field where the massacre occurred. I reflect on this experience in the poem "Beneath the Pagoda's Perch" in *Love and Injustice in Medicine* (Iguana Books, 2022).

[144] Kennedy convinced Soviet leader Nikita Khrushchev to dismantle the missiles planted in Cuba (https://www.jfklibrary.org/learn/about-jfk/jfk-in-history/cuban-missile-crisis). Kennedy also refused to send in American troops to support the Cuban-American expats stranded on the beach at the Bay of Pigs after attempting to retake Cuba in 1961 from Fidel Castro's revolutionaries (*The Bay of Pigs: The Untold Story* (1980) by Peter Wyden).

[145] The Civil Rights Bill made discrimination illegal in education, including in schools in the American South. President Kennedy was assassinated before he could sign this Bill into law, but his Vice President Lyndon Johnson, who was a Southerner, surprisingly carried through with Kennedy's Bill when he became President. In addition, Johnson eventually signed Kennedy's "Voting Rights Bill."

Or Kennedy's support for Dr. King[146]
In King's quest to desegregate schools in Alabama
Where the President did send in troops
To ensure desegregation occurred smoothly
I remember watching the Evening News on Channel 4
And seeing Alabama's Governor George Wallace
Standing in a doorway at the University of Alabama
Refusing to permit Black students to enter[147]

I remember watching a film on Malcom X[148]
Who had criticized fellow Black Muslims for mourning a white President's death
And was admonished by his leader Elijah Muhammad
Because "Everybody loved the man"
I was one of the "Everybody loved the man"
As President Kennedy was my high school hero[149]
And whenever I'm invited to speak in Washington

---

[146] Dr. Martin Luther King Jr. was assassinated in 1968 in Memphis Tennessee, where he had gone to support a sanitation-workers strike (https://www.washingtonpost.com/news/retropolis/wp/2018/02/12/i-am-a-man-the-1968-memphis-sanitation-workers-strike-that-led-to-mlks-assassination/). Dr. King's casket was symbolically pulled by mules, rather than by beautiful horses like President Kennedy's casket had been pulled five years before.

[147] George Wallace's confrontation at this door is captured in the Academy Award-winning film *Forrest Gump* (1994), directed by Robert Zemeckis, starring Tom Hanks.

[148] The film 1992 *Malcolm X*, starring Denzel Washington in the title role, was directed and co-written by Spike Lee. Malcolm X was assassinated in 1965. Elijah Muhammad, the leader of the Black Muslims, and thus the spiritual and political leader of hundreds of thousands of Americans, was accused of contracting the death of Malcolm X, because the views of Malcolm X had become too much like President Kennedy's, focusing on equality rather than difference, compassion rather than militancy.

[149] President Kennedy was also a war hero. As Captain of PT 109, he swam back and forth from his sinking ship to a Japanese-held island, pulling injured crew members behind him. The film PT 109 (1963) was directed by Leslie H. Martinson and Lewis Milestone, and starred Cliff Robertson as a young John Kennedy.

I always pilgrimage to the President's grave in Arlington

I solemnly walk through the cemetery's gates
And slowly up the road to the eternal flame
Where I kneel at the President's grave
Across the path from where his brother Robert lay[150]
And surrounded by thousands of white crosses
Planted in the decade after the President's death
Marking the graves of soldiers killed in Vietnam
In a war Kennedy had condemned

Kennedy's beacon leads me to this day
And hopefully encourages courage[151] in my generation
And hopeful will in future generations
Hopefully committed to the social justice the President believed in
And ask not what their country can do for them[152]
Rather what they can do for persons in their country
And ask what they can do to achieve equality
And ask what they can do to achieve peace

---

[150] Robert Kennedy was assassinated in 1968 during his campaign for the presidency. Three months later Dr. Martin Luther King Jr. was assassinated.
[151] When John Kennedy was a student at Harvard University, he wrote the book *Profiles in Courage*, acknowledging those whose courage inspired him.
[152] Paraphrased from John F Kennedy's inaugural address in which he said, "Ask not what your country can do for you, ask what you can do for your country."

Chapter 11

Marabeth the Best of Us

Marabeth was the best of us
The best of girl friends
In the true sense of the word "friend"
Rather than anyone's exclusive "girlfriend"
Marabeth was the best musician of us
A gift to Mr. Perkins[153] on flute or piano
And always eager to assist him with
The much-less-talented rest of us

Indeed Marabeth was generous with her gift with us
Always present with effervescent enthusiasm
Not to mention unlimited patience
Making music more fun for the rest of us
Marabeth's music gift was perhaps genetic
Probably inherited from her father
"First Viola" in the Toronto Symphony Orchestra
And from "old country" musicians of previous generations[154]

---

[153] See Chapter 4 "Favourite Teacher Mr. Perkins."
[154] "Old country" music still exists in "klezmer" bands at some Jewish weddings, remarkably similar to the band featured in Norman Jewison's Oscar-winning film *Fiddler on the Roof* (1971).

Marabeth was the best debater of us
And I had the gift of being her partner
Until Senior Year when our English teacher
Prohibited us from being together
He said it was unfair to the other students
We refuted separating us was unfair to us
Because our goal was not to win our school championship
But to win the City of Toronto championship

Neither Marabeth or I thought we could win it
Without the partnership of each other
But the teacher assigned us other partners
And Marabeth's new partner was Gail[155]
Marabeth's team beat my team in our school's finals
And indeed went on to win the City Championship
Revealing the undebatable fact
That it was Marabeth who was the star debater

Marabeth and I were never amorous
As even the thought of it seemed incestuous
Though we did dance together frenetically
To the frantic songs at our Friday Night Dances[156]
However we never danced slow songs together
After the one slow dance we attempted
And I still remember the thin lace of Marabeth's black blouse
And how awkward I felt sensing the skin of her lower back

We lost track of each other after graduation
As Marabeth travelled as a much-sought-after musician
While I remained in Toronto to do medical school[157]

---

[155] See Chapter 15 "The Girl Everyone Thought I Would Marry."
[156] See Chapter 2 "Friday Night Dances."
[157] You could achieve "direct entry" from high school into the six-year Pre Med/Med program at U of T.

As my old-world inheritance demanded I do[158]
And after med school I went to London
To do my residency with a famous cancer surgeon[159]
And a PhD and started a family
And lost track of Marabeth too easily

In retrospect I didn't seek her hard enough
Though I often wondered where Marabeth was
Especially when I blew my guts out on my sax[160]
Knowing the limit of my talent compared to Marabeth's
Recently Allan[161] the person in our class
Who actually kept track of the rest of us
Invited me to "a gathering" at Mr. Perkins's[162] home
And as usual I responded "I'll call in"

And while I was speaking to Mr. Perkins
I was sure I heard Marabeth's voice in the distance
For more than several impatient minutes
Before Mr. Perkins said "Jeff here's Marabeth"
Marabeth's voice evaporated a half-century
And as we eagerly caught up on the phone
I sensed the skin of her lower back in my hands
Like I did during our one slow dance

---

[158] In the "old country" one boy in each generation was chosen to go to medical school. My father was so chosen, but the Holocaust prohibited his attendance (See "You Must Go to Medical School or Hitler Will Have Won" *In* Nisker J. Love and Injustice in Medicine, Iguana Books, 2022).

[159] I reflect on Dr. Hugh Allen in "I'm Sorry Vaccine Came Too Late for You Janet" (Nisker J. Love and Injustice in Medicine, Iguana Books, 2022).

[160] I played clarinet in Mr. Perkins's orchestra (See Chapter 4 "Favourite Teacher Mr. Perkins"), but switched to tenor sax to play in a physician rock band.

[161] See Chapter 16 "Always Serious Allan."

[162] See Chapter 4 "Favourite Teacher Mr. Perkins."

Chapter 12

Wild Mrs. Rose[163]

Mrs. Rose may have been the inspiration of
"The Little Old Lady From Pasadena"[164]
Though Mrs. Rose drove a shiny-red Corvette[165]
Not a "shiny-red super stock Dodge"
And though Mr. Rose lived in Toronto
Not in Pasadena California
She was just as the song goes
"Go granny go granny go granny go"

Mrs. Rose was nearing retirement
When I sat in her Senior math class
At the opposite end of our high school

---

[163] The wild rose is the emblem of Canada's Province of Alberta. I fondly use the adjective "wild" to describe Mrs. Rose, though I doubt she was from Alberta because of her English accent.

[164] Written by Don Altfeld, Jan Berry and Roger Christian, recorded by Jan and Dean. The song hit the air waves when I was a senior in high school.

[165] Mrs. Rose's red Corvette may have also been the inspiration for the red Corvette of The Artist Known as Prince in his song "Give Me a Red Corvette." Perhaps he saw Mrs. Rose bombing down Minneapolis way.

From Mr. Perkins's music room[166]
The opposite was also reflected
In Mrs. Rose's opposite demeanour
From Mr. Perkins's warmth and kindness
That Mrs. Rose possessed but kept hidden

Mrs. Rose had to stretch to be five feet
So her omnipotent presence was achieved
By the snap of her vicious yardstick
That demanded quiet in her class
And also in the halls when we rotated between classes
As we clung tightly to the halls' walls
While Mrs. Rose strolled down their middles
Nipping the shoulders of talkers or strayers

Mrs. Rose parked her shiny red Corvette
In the teacher's lot near Mr. Fennel's portable[167]
But none of us dared go near it
Let alone touch its high-gloss finish
We just admired Mrs. Rose's 'Vette from the distance
Acknowledging it the "sweetest ride" we'd ever seen
And the 'Vette added prestige to Mrs. Rose
Though "sweetest" was an adjective that didn't go

Mrs. Rose sat me behind Erle[168]
Our province's most brilliant student
Hoping Erle's genius was contagious
But I of course was more realistic
As repeatedly proven when Mrs. Rose entered us
In math competitions at Waterloo University
Which in my case just wasted Saturdays
When I could have been busily sleeping the day away

---

[166] See Chapter 4 "Favourite Teacher Mr. Perkins."
[167] See Chapter 10 "High School's Darkest Day."
[168] See Chapter 7 "Brilliant Erle."

There was a long tradition in our high school
Of returning exam papers in reverse order
Of the red grade engraved on the front page[169]
Thus of course Erle always had to wait
This manner of returning papers was brutal
And I felt awful for my friends with bowed heads
Silently begging their teacher pass them by
At least for a little while longer

When Mrs. Rose returned our mid-term papers
We could tell she was terribly upset
So we all slipped our hands under our thick math texts
To protect them from her yardstick
And hoped Mrs. Rose would pass our desk
Until she only had a few papers left
Reserved for Erle and the next best
Another tradition we had come to expect

Yet this day Mrs. Rose's scowl
Was even more brutal than usual
And her face was as red as the Xs on our papers
But I was fortunate mine was second last
However Mrs. Rose hovered over my desk
Glaring at the back of Erle's brilliant head
Then picked up my math textbook and smashed it on that head
Which hit his desk and rebounded for second smash

The class gasped in unison
And it was lucky for Erle that Mrs. Rose didn't weigh much
Or there would have been blood all over his desk
Not to mention a smashed-in head
Erle was of course frightened

---

[169] See Chapter 19 "Mr. Kerr's Antics."

And his brilliance kept his head on his desk
While he whispered to Mrs. Rose
"What did I do to deserve that"

Mrs. Rose shouted back
"It's what you didn't do you fool"
And Erle's genius kept his head on his desk
While Mrs. Rose continued
"In my 40 years as a teacher
I've never marked a perfect paper
And you denied me this with a punctuation error
How could you be so incredibly stupid"

Then Mrs. Rose lost it completely on Erle
Culminating in "Get out of my class"
And flabbergasted Erle left the class quickly
Never having been kicked out of a class previously
Unlike me whose occasional clevernesses
Was interpreted by teachers as disrespect
Prompting a similar kicked-out fate
But Erle was always so well behaved

I still reflect warmly on Mrs. Rose
Whenever a Corvette growls past
Though 'Vettes seem a bit rarer now
And driven mostly by male seniors
But 'Vettes are still predominantly red
Making it easy for me to reminisce
A wild rose like Mrs. Rose
Almost my favourite teacher[170]

---

[170] Mr. Perkins was my favourite teacher (See Chapter 4 "Favourite Teacher Mr. Perkins"), and second favourite was Miss Kingsbury for very different reasons (See Chapter 1 "Miss Kingsbury Teaches Comprehension").

Chapter 13

York Memo Girl

Our basketball team squeezed across the back seats
Of the three Diamond Taxis[171] idling in the street
At the front entrance of our high school
With instructions to deliver us to York Memorial[172]
It was the last game of the regular season
And we had already clinched a play-off berth
And a win would not alter our third-place position
But of course we still wanted to win

York Memo was an annually weak team
So there was little anticipation and less trepidation
As we exited our cabs at York Memo's front entrance
Carved in an identical cement façade to ours[173]

---

[171] Diamond Taxis were black with an orange roof, on which a horizontal white-diamond light proclaimed "Diamond." Diamond Taxis were more common than Yellow Cabs in Toronto when I was in high school.
[172] York Memorial Collegiate was in the northwest corner of our district.
[173] Many of the older high schools in Toronto had identical cement façades surrounding their front doors.

There we were met by a Phys Ed teacher[174]
Who led us down a corridor we'd been down before
Passing classrooms to where we knew
"Boys Change Room" would appear soon

However this year I stopped abruptly
And gasped through a classroom's open front door[175]
Transfixed by an amazingly attractive girl
As beautiful as Tamarra[176] but with dark hair
The York Memo girl was staring at the blackboard
From the front desk of the second row
And I was magnetically immobilized by her eyes
Even before she turned her head and noticed mine

My lovely trance was only broken
When I was elbowed forward by Allan[177]
Who taunted "C'mon lover boy
Remember we've got a game to play"
His shove almost caused me to trip
As my feet were firmly cemented
And had no intention of moving an inch
While I was drinking in such lovely absinthe[178]

My lungs were hyperventilating
And my heart beating rapidly
Even before I ran my first fast break
And indeed I had forgotten "We've got a game to play"
It took our coach's "Get going Nisker

---

[174] We could tell he was a Phys Ed teacher by his brush-cut and attire, right down to his white Converse All-Star basketball shoes (See Chapter 6 "Black Chucks").

[175] Classrooms had front doors to exit and back doors to enter.

[176] See Chapter 27 "Queen Tamarra."

[177] See Chapter 16 "Always Serious Allan."

[178] Absinthe is the nectar loved by the Greek gods.

Get changed or you're not going to start"
Before I reluctantly joined our team's stream
Funneling into the boys change room

When we ran our warm-up layups
I missed some because I wasn't looking at the basket
Rather looking at the students filtering into the stands
Searching for a beautiful one of them
And when we took our warm-up jump shots
I was hit in the head by a high chest pass
As my eyes were fixed on the filling bleachers
Having already checked out the six cheerleaders

When I dribbled up the court for the first time
I again swept the bleachers with my eyes
Hoping the potential love-of-my-life
Had finally decided to come to the game
But after my third time up the court
And our coach's third "Nisker focus"
I gave up on the wondrous girl appearing
Though I remained riveted on her for months

The next year was my Senior Year of high school
And I was selected by our Vice Principal
To be our high school's "Eaton's Rep"[179]
With his advice to accept this "honour and privilege"
Eaton's was sponsoring a Leadership Program
On Saturday mornings at its Eaton's College Street store[180]
For "promising students" it hoped would promise
To work summers for Eaton's on the road to becoming Execs

---

[179] Eaton's Downtown on Yonge between Queen and Dundas, across from the Imperial Theatre (See Chapter 8 "Rag Doll") was Canada's largest department store.
[180] Eaton's College St. was known for its fashions and luncheons for wealthy women (See Chapter 27 "Queen Tamarra").

Of course I had better things to do on Saturday mornings
Than being groomed to be an Exec
Such as sleeping in or playing basketball
Or even listening to Mozart in the Central Library[181]
Yet this clearly-not-great debater[182]
Could not talk my way out of
The "honour and privilege" of being selected
To be our high school's "Eaton's Rep"

As I entered the splendorous Eaton's Auditorium
For our first Saturday morning encounter
I saw almost 100 students already sitting there
Eager to see Canada's greatest hockey player
Gordie Howe[183] walked on the stage to applause
And modestly shook hands with the Eaton's Execs
And even though Gordie was in a jacket and tie
He was easily recognizable above their heads

After all his face was the most famous in Canada
From TV's "Hockey Night in Canada"[184]
However after a quick glance at the impressive Gordie
My eyes were more impressed with the York Memo girl
She was walking down the auditorium's centre aisle
And decided to sit in empty row three
Where she was immediately joined by me
Though I respectfully left three seats between us

I nodded at her and murmured
"I'm sure you go to York Memo"

---

[181] Final Year music was not offered at our high school, so I listened to the symphonies on the curriculum through a headset in a wingback chair at the Central Library.
[182] See Chapter 11 "Marabeth the Best of Us."
[183] Wayne Gretzky had not yet been imagined.
[184] "Hockey Night in Canada" was a ritual for Canadian boys and even men.

She turned her head and shyly smiled
Which was all I needed to slide right beside her
The York Memo girl was even more beautiful up close
And I swam in the sea of her deep green eyes
Then extended my right hand and softly said
"I'm glad to meet you my name is Jeff"

She gently took my hand and lifted her eyes
Shyly smiled again and whispered
"My name is Teressa I'm surprised you recognized me"
I opened my mouth but nothing came out
I must admit I have no recollection
Of hockey's greatest at the podium
As my eyes were adhered to Teressa
And my ears perked for her slightest whisper

Teressa felt my eyes and ears on her
And she couldn't stop her skin from reddening
And I'm sure she heard my heart thumping
Drowning out Gordie's microphoned voice
When that morning's Eaton's Rep session ended
Teressa and I walked out of the Aud together
And I asked her if I could drive her home
But she said she was staying downtown to buy a gift for her father

Of course I offered to shop with her
Assuring I could be helpful being a guy and all
Although admitting to being a terrible shopper
Teressa blushed but said "No thank you"
Not one to give up when smitten
I fumbled "May I at least ask you out for tonight?"
Teressa more worried than shy replied
"I'm sorry but I can't go out with you tonight"

My heart dropped as I asked Teressa

"Do you have a boyfriend or something?"
Teressa quizzically looked at me shaking her head
Then laughingly said "No"
The next Saturday I arrived at the Aud early
To ensure I could sit beside Teressa
Which I rapidly did as soon as she sat down
And she turned her head after my "Hi Teressa"

Then to my ecstatic heart's flip
Teressa whispered "Hi Jeff"
She remembered my name that had to be a good thing
This time it was my turn to blush
I silently begged Teressa's remembrance of my name
Was unrelated to the adhesive name tag
Stuck on the left lapel of my black blazer
Just above my rapidly-beating heart

I have no recollection of the guest speaker
But I do remember Teressa and I speaking after he was finished
And asking her "Are you coming to the dance tonight?"
And holding my breath for her answer
Eaton's was sponsoring a dance in the auditorium
Following an ensemble performance of Toronto Symphony musicians
To further hook its "Reps" for future allegiance
On the path to becoming Eaton's Execs

Teressa looked at me for what seemed more than a minute
But was probably just a few seconds
Then said "Jeff I usually don't go to dances"
So I pleaded "Teressa please make an exception"
Teressa swallowed hard before saying
"I'll come to the dance but it's not like a date or anything"
Of course I ignored "not like a date or anything"
And asked Teressa for her address

Teressa's left hand grazed my right hand
And her voltage zapped my brain
But she said "Let's just meet at the dance
And remember it's not like a date or anything"
As you may have guessed I came to the dance early
And eagerly waited on the street for Teressa
And literally felt my heart exploding
As open-mouthed I watched her approaching

I opened the door and helped Teressa off with her coat
And hung it on a long aluminum coat-rack
Then followed Teressa down the centre aisle
Enamoured by the freckles on her lovely back
Eaton's had set up tiny tables
Between the stage and the Aud's seats
And on that stage twenty musicians waited
For the great Seigi[185] to lead them

Teressa paused and shyly looked at me
As if she wanted me to suggest at which table to sit
But I just kept smiling at Teressa
Too much resembling the Cheshire Cat[186]
Teressa rolled her eyes then gracefully claimed
One of the tiny tables with her purse
Tables so tiny our heads almost touched
And I could inhale her lovely breath

---

[185] Seiji Ozawa was the conductor of the Toronto Symphony Orchestra from 1965 to 1969, and conductor of the San Francisco Symphony Orchestra from 1970 to 1976. He then became conductor of the Boston Symphony Orchestra.
[186] The "Cheshire Cat" is a character from *Alice's Adventures in Wonderland* by Lewis Carroll.

The dancing was soon to get underway
On the Aud's balloon-embossed stage
In a space roped-off in front of
The great Seiji's ensemble orchestra
I don't remember which Exec welcomed us
Or the slightest idea of what he said
As my consciousness was fully concentrated
On restraining my hand from Teressa's till we danced

After eons the dancing started
And I was cautious not to hold Teressa too close
In the too-few-not-slow-enough slow dances
While hoping for more and more slow dances
Dancing with Teressa was wonderful
And I never considered dancing with another partner
Perhaps never dancing with another partner ever
If that was what Teressa wanted

But Seigi was also enamoured with Teressa
And chose her frequently as his dance partner
But I kept cutting in so Teressa could be all mine
Even though she wasn't my "date or anything"
After a couple of hours of Teressa and I growing closer
With each of the too-few-not-slow-enough slow dances
One of the Execs announced with regret
That it was past eleven and the dance had to end

Teressa collected her purse from our table
And we walked slowly up the Aud's centre aisle
To the coat-rack where I even more slowly
Helped Teressa on with her coat
Then I asked her if I could drive her home
Instead of her having to take a taxi[187]

---

[187] Eaton's even paid for taxis.

I didn't want our wondrous evening to end
But if it had to I wanted it ending with a kiss

Teressa looked up at me with saddening eyes
Took a deep breath and shook her head
Then touched my left arm and hesitantly whispered
"Jeff I don't think you should"
Rather than being disappointed
Although I'm sure I was and more than a bit
I was also surprised by Teressa's reply
And cautiously whispered "Why not?"

"Jeff I don't think you're a Catholic
And I'm only allowed to go out with Catholic boys"
Without missing a heartbeat I said "I can convert"
But my words were not humourous to Teressa
How Teressa knew I wasn't "a Catholic"
Will always remain a mystery to me
As although Eaton's provided us with name tags
They didn't mention our religion or lack thereof

However my given name isn't Seamus or Liam
Or Sean or Tony or even Ian
And my last name isn't prefixed with
An O' or Mc or Fitz
Teressa swallowed hard before looking up at me
Saying "Jeff I'm so terribly sorry"
And it wasn't till that moment I noticed
The silver cross under the top buttons of her blouse

It felt like Teressa's cross was meant to repel me
As if I was a vampire in a Dracula movie
But I softly hugged her cross against my chest
And after a minute I had the breath to whisper
"Teressa this is too good to let religion

Prevent us from being together"
Teressa's woodenness released my hug
And her discomfort nudged me backward

Teressa's green eyes looked up at me
Silently speaking "There's nothing I can do"
And the longer our eyes caressed each others
The more Teressa's filled with tears
And the more my shoulders lowered
And the more my lungs collapsed
There were no words to express what just happened
Just because I wasn't "a Catholic"

Teressa would not permit me to drive her home
So I walked her to a Yellow Cab on College Street
And opened its curbside back door for her
But before I closed it I heard her address
And thought I might mention next Saturday
That she only lived about twenty minutes from me
However Teressa didn't come to next Saturday's session
Indeed I never saw Teressa again

Even though I knew Teressa's address
I thought it rude to just knock on her door
And intrude the non-Catholic me
Into the rules she was living under
Yet Teressa haunted me with longing and warmth
And the following autumn I confess looking for her
In the cafeteria of St. Michael's College[188]
Even though St. Mike's was on the far end of campus

However the long walk would have been worth it

---

[188] St. Michael's College is the Catholic College at the University of Toronto.

If I could have been with Teressa again
For I still find myself thinking about "The York Memo Girl"
Obviously more intensely while I'm writing this poem
On the complications of Teressa's religion
And my profound lack of religion
And our abbreviated and uncompleted
High school love story

Chapter 14

Solid Paul

Paul was the most solid of us
Always standing up for what was just
He was the guy you wanted beside you
In park disturbances and street skirmishes
Paul once ripped a large guy off me so hard
The aggressor sprawled unconscious on the sidewalk
Yet Paul was smaller than I was
Except for his muscles and his heart

Paul lived at the distant end of our block
In a modern house of glass and wood
Anomalous amidst the brick "cookie-cutters"
In our inner-suburb neighbourhood
Also anomalous Paul's mother drove a Peugeot
The only Peugeot I would ever know
Because "What's good for General Motors
Is good for the USA"[189]

---

[189] Frequent TV commercial slogan when I was in high school. "Good for the USA" also meant good for Canada in my high school days. My father

I was always quiet while in Paul's house
As it seemed more dignified than ours was
Perhaps because of his father's English accent
Or his mother's non-plastic-covered furniture
Even in her elegant living room
That we were actually allowed to go in
While hoping to be asked for dinner
Of her delicious cheeseburgers with a glass of milk[190]

Paul went to school earlier than the rest of us
Because of his pre-dawn swim practices
Or his pre-dawn detentions for not finishing assignments
Because Paul was also in the pool after school
Except when Paul was playing pool
In the pool hall just West of our high school
Paul's swim practices permitted city championships
Paul detentions permitted graduation

Paul was also good in other sports
Including playing quarterback on our football team[191]
But Paul played illegally because the parents on our street had agreed
Not to sign permission forms for fear of head injuries[192]
But lack of parental consent didn't stop Paul
He just forged his father's signature and was a star

---

and uncles drove GM cars. In 2025, American President Donald Trump used "Good for the USA" philosophy to inflict tariffs on all Canadian-manufactured vehicles. The tariffs included vehicles from the enormous GM plant in Oshawa just east of Toronto, that once employed thousands of Canadians.

[190] There were no dietary restrictions in Paul's house.

[191] After Frank dropped out to work full-time because Suzy was pregnant (See Chapter 3 "Frank and Suzy").

[192] Frequently warned of in the press.

Until his father read in "The Toronto Star"[193]
That Paul was selected an "All City All Star"

Paul's football career instantly ended
And he was fortunate he wasn't suspended
And I was fortunate he was permitted basketball
Which was a more important sport after all
Paul either played third-guard beside Salvatore[194] and me
Or small-forward subbing for Mark[195] or Allan[196]
Paul's abdominals made up for his height disadvantage
Suspending him in the air as if by magic

Paul married a wonderful girl named Wendy
Who we all thought was just awesome
But awesome didn't stop Wendy from dying young
From metastatic ovarian cancer
Wendy's blonde hair and blue eyes
Spoke of a different heritage than ours
Considered a threat by my tradition-burdened father[197]
Even though he wasn't the slightest bit religious

Of course my friends and I didn't take religion seriously[198]
Having thrown off its shackles in our early teens
And vowing religion would never restrict us again
Yet religion did restrict me three years after graduation
When I was smitten with the love-of-my-life Gwendolyn[199]
Who insisted on being called Gwen
And arguments with my father about seeing no difference

---

[193] *The Toronto Star* was our most widely read newspaper in Canada when we were in high school.
[194] See Chapter 5 "Friendly Salvatore."
[195] See Chapter 9 "High School Best Friend Mark."
[196] See Chapter 16 "Always Serious Allan."
[197] See Afterward "Mr. Perkins and Gwendolyn."
[198] See Chapter 13 "York Memo Girl."
[199] See Afterward "Mr. Perkins and Gwendolyn."

Caused a schism that would be permanent

When I would go to Guelph to visit Paul and Wendy
Wendy would always greet me with a big hug
During which I would ask her to tell me a story[200]
Or I would just start singing "Windy"[201]

When Wendy developed ovarian cancer
She called me to learn more about her treatment
And I drove to Guelph to see her immediately
Following which we spoke on the phone frequently
After Wendy's death whenever I visited Paul
I was engulfed by the emptiness of their home
Though remnants of Wendy's living were hanging everywhere
And lay scattered on sink counters

There was no air left in their home
In the vacuum of Wendy's absence
And Paul's loneliness was excruciating
But all I could do was hug the no longer solid Paul
We all loved Wendy dearly
And thought Paul was lucky to be married to her
Wendy was so warm and generous
Why was she the first to have to leave us

---

[200] In *Peter Pan* by E.M. Barrie, Wendy told her brothers stories to help them go to sleep. Eventually Peter Pan flew Wendy to Neverland to tell the Lost Boys bedtime stories, and she even brought her brothers along.
[201] "Windy" was a hit song by I think The Association (1967), songwriter Ruthann Friedman.

Chapter 15

The Girl Everyone Thought I

Would Marry

Gail was another high school girlfriend
With emphasis on friend in its most platonic sense[202]
Except Gail was the girl I was sure I would marry
And Gail was the girl who was sure she would marry me
Indeed everyone in our Senior Year
Were sure Gail and I would marry
But first we needed to be "going steady"
Instead of just being each other's Prom dates[203]

Gail's enthusiasm was so infectious
It secured her a cheerleader gig
Even though Gail was too tall for flips
And her voice too quiet for cheers
Gail's intelligence secured her a seat

---

[202] See Chapter 11 "Marabeth the Best of Us."
[203] See Chapter 26 "The Prom."

Between Erle and me on "Reach for the Top"[204]
And Gail and I hung our heads together
When we narrowly and perhaps unfairly[205] lost

Gail lived near the opposite end of our street from Paul[206]
On the brick apex of "the hill"[207]
And I'd go out of my way to dribble by her house occasionally
And run by it more than just occasionally
Because if Gail was out front I would stop
And we would solve the problems of the universe on her curb
Until one day Gail stared at me with her bluish-gray eyes and said
"Why don't you ever ask me out except for the Prom"

Her question hit me like a rogue wave
Because I never thought of Gail in a date way
But of course I promptly responded
"Let's go to movie on Saturday"
We went to the Bayview Cinema[208]
To see *The Umbrellas of Cherbourg*[209]

---

[204] "Reach for the Top" was a TV competition between teams of four high school students; sort of a team version of *Jeopardy* (https://www.reachforthetop.com/).

[205] After the warm-up round in which we slaughtered our opponents, New Testament questions were added to the round that would be broadcast on television. We had been told to try hard in the warm-up round because it might indeed be the round that counted if there was a technical glitch in the round planned to be counted.

[206] See Chapter 14 "Solid Paul."

[207] Indeed the street was called Chiltern Hill. Long before I was in high school, brick had been employed on hills frequently rather than asphalt to prevent cracking in winter.

[208] The Bayview Cinema would be refurbished and rebranded Bayview Playhouse.

[209] *The Umbrellas of Cherbourg* is a French operatic film, written and directed by Jacques Demy, that came to Canadian cinemas around 1968. I am reminded of this film whenever I watch World War II films that open with the Normandy Invasion such as *Saving Private Ryan* (1998) directed by Steven Spielberg and starring Tom Hanks, as Cherbourg was an

The best "foreign language"[210] film I had ever seen
And to this day have ever seen[211]

However sitting beside Gail was distracting
As I kept wondering whether I should I touch her arm
And I felt relief when she rose from her seat
Saying excuse me "I need the loo"
But my relief soon dissipated
Because Gail was in the bathroom a long time
And I became concerned that she was ill
And started walking up the theatre's hill

Just as Gail began to descend it
And graciously smiled at me
A smile that had me debating on the drive home
Whether to suggest a goodnight kiss
However at Gail's door I decided against this
As a kiss could be misinterpreted
So Gail pecked my cheek instead
Then put her hands on my shoulders

And stared at me with those bluish-gray eyes
Seeming surprised I didn't take the initiative
And asked "Is everything all right?"
And I responded "Absolutely" cautiously smiling
Then Gail asked "Do you want to play tennis tomorrow?"
And added "You'll have to bring an extra racquet"
And added "And teach me to play of course"
And added "I've never played tennis before"

---

important deep-water port that the allies fought hard to take in order to retake
Europe. A very young Catherine Deneuve sings the lead.

[210] I place "foreign language" within quotation marks, as the film won an
Oscar in this category; however, French is not a foreign language in Canada.

[211] The Spanish film *Pan's Labyrinth* (2006), the Greek film *Z* (1969) and
the German film *Run Lola Run* (1998) are close seconds.

I picked up Gail the next morning
And drove to the Winston Churchill Tennis Courts
And I teased "You're wearing Bermuda shorts
Which will make tennis tougher of course"
Gail asked me if there was a dress code
Probably because her shorts were maroon
Not white like mine were and everyone else's would be
Like on the courts on TV during high school

I responded "I don't think there's a dress code
Because the courts are supposed to be public"
And added "I don't give a damn anyway
The worse that can happen is some stiff kicks us off"
Gail seemed pleased and touched my knee
But her touch reminded me I had to be careful
Because a movie or tennis or Prom[212]
Was very different from "going steady"

Yet I admired Gail completely
Her kindness and intelligence and caring
And was sure like everyone else
That one day Gail and I would marry
However I wasn't close to even being ready
To contemplate "going steady"
Let alone with a girl I not only considered a friend
But had future wife written all over her[213]

---

[212] See Chapter 26 "The Prom."

[213] After we graduated high school, Gail pursued an undergraduate degree at the University of Toronto, while Sam and I took early entry to Med School (See Chapter 28 "Gillda and Sam"). Sam lived the furthest north and would always pick up Gillda and Gail before me. I can still feel the texture of Gail's softly-plaided wool slacks that she wore in winter, as I squished in beside her in the back of Sam's car.

I graduated Med School the year before Gail entered
And moved to London to do work with a famous cancer surgeon[214]
And lost track of Gail and she lost track of me
And marrying Gail became a lost possibility
We entered relationships and had children
And immersed ourselves in the practice of medicine
And it was twenty years before I saw Gail again
After a talk I gave at a Conference in Victoria

I was blown away seeing Gail
And hugged her longer than appropriate
And she hugged me back longer than appropriate
Then put her hands on my shoulders and stared with those bluish-
gray eyes
And we caught up over coffee
Talking of things other than what might have been
Careful not to let nostalgia take over
In spite of the spell we were under

---

[214] Dr. Hugh Allen.

Chapter 16

Always Serious Allan

Allan is the persistent cement
That sticks the rest of us together
Allan is the forever friend
Who never smiles but is always present
Allan lived near where my grandparents had lived
In an older neighbourhood just north of St. Clair
In fact my mother grew up in that neighbourhood
Recently gentrified to excess after Allan had left

Allan played power-forward on our basketball team
Setting solid "picks"[215] for this skinnier guard
And helping Mark[216] and Saul[217] on the backboards
Rarely being selfish enough to score
And whether or not we won or lost
Allan's lack of smiling was consistent
Except perhaps for a suppressed grin
Allan would permit us after a big win

---

[215] A "pick" is the procedure in which a player stands firm while his teammate brushes his cover off him.
[216] See Chapter 9 "High School Best Friend Mark."
[217] See Chapter 24 "Tall Saul."

Allan was one of the cat-disturbers
In Mr. Perkins's orchestra[218]
One of the few that Mr. Perkins
Never had to ask to "tune up"
One day Allan took his violin from under his chin
And started plucking its strings transversely
But as we had no music for a guitar
Mr. Perkins suggested stand-up bass

Mr. Perkins's suggestion was Allan's true music beginning
And a half-century later there is no ending
As Allan is playing bass guitar professionally
In some of Canada's greatest rock bands[219]
Allan also has a solo music career
As a singer and songwriter[220]
Touring North America and beyond
With his guitar and his songs

Allan's music gift was perhaps genetic
As his father was the assistant Cantor
At Canada's largest synagogue
And chanted the first hour of Saturday services
To empty seats[221] except for at least ten men
Needed to be there for a *minyan*
Most of whom were there to say *Kaddish*
The Jewish prayer for the dead

---

[218] See Chapter 4 "Favourite Teacher Mr. Perkins."
[219] Allan toured the world as Dan Hill's bass guitarist (https://sobermanmusic.com/bio)
[220] "Still My Father's Son" (https://sobermanmusic.com/pullin-up-the-covers)
[221] The enormous main sanctuary of Beth Tzedec was only populated during the High Holidays.

At ten o'clock Allan's father turned over the podium
To the "Head Cantor" who had survived "the camps"[222]
Because even the Nazis didn't want to destroy
The purity of his high tenor voice
My friends and I had no choice but to hear his voice
At least during the High Holidays
Albeit through the closed doors of the sanctuary
While we played soccer in the foyer[223] with a milk container

The last time I saw Allan was at a three-person get-together
Allan arranged at Paul's[224] home
A get-together I was hesitant to attend
Because Wendy would not be there[225]
I hugged Paul long and hard as I entered
As there was no getting over Wendy's death
Then I hugged Allan and thanked him
For putting together this get-together

The last time I spoke with Allan was over the phone
When he called me from Mr. Perkins's home[226]
During a get-together I couldn't attend
And his last words were "Here's Mr. Perkins"[227]
Then Allan as was always his practice
Set himself in the background
Preferring to be a support person
Rather than the superstar that was Allan

---

[222] "The camps" refers to Hitler's concentration camps like Auschwitz-Birkenau and Treblinka, where six million Jewish persons perished.
[223] We would also play football in the parking lot, including the annual "Yom Kippur Bowl," during which we often tore our dress pants on the cement.
[224] See Chapter 14 "Solid Paul."
[225] Paul's wife, Wendy, had recently died from ovarian cancer (See Chapter 14 "Solid Paul").
[226] See Chapter 4 "Favourite Teacher Mr. Perkins."
[227] Mr. Perkins soon passed the phone over to Marabeth (See Chapter 11 "Marabeth the Best of Us").

Chapter 17

Quiet Sid

Sid was the shyest of us
Which is why he was the quietest of us
And Sid was also different from the rest of us
In that his parents had gone to university
In fact Sid's father was a physician
The only physician in our neighbourhood
Thus Sid lived in the largest house of us
With our neighbourhood's only colour television[228]

Sid often walked to high school with Mark[229] and I
Though it meant half a kilometre out of his way
And Sid's shyness mitigated girl-talk
So Sid was silent all the way
Sid would remain silent about girls
Through all our years of high school
Though Mark and I kept trying to fix him up
But at the last minute heard "Something's come up"

---

[228] I was blown away the New Years Day when I first watched Sid's colour television during the Rose Bowl.

[229] See Chapter 9 "High School Best Friend Mark."

Sid studied harder than the rest of us
Because he wanted to be a doctor like his father
He even studied weeks in advance of exams
And deep into the night during exam week
Sid was a positive influence on this less-motivated friend
Who didn't believe in studying in advance
But did cram the night before exams
As long as I could see Sid's lamp in the distance

Sid being such a serious student
Did allow him to follow in his father's footsteps
Starting with Western University
For his undergraduate degree
Then Sid attended Med School at Western
Further keeping up his family tradition[230]
Except Sid specialized in quiet Radiology[231]
Conversing silently with x-ray films

Six years after high school graduation[232]
I moved to London and joined Sid at Western
But for me it was to work with a famous cancer surgeon[233]
Because of my mother's family tradition[234]

---

[230] My father's family tradition was also medicine in pre-holocaust Poland, with one son in each generation chosen to attend medical school. My father was so chosen, but the Holocaust prevented his attendance (See "You Must Go to Medical School or Hitler Will Have Won" *In* Nisker, *Love and Injustice in Medicine*, Iguana Books, 2022).

[231] Sid's father was an Allergist.

[232] In these six years I did Pre Meds and Meds at the University of Toronto.

[233] Dr. Hugh Allen (See "I'm Sorry Vaccine Came Too Late for You Janet" *In* Nisker, *Love and Injustice in Medicine*, Iguana Books, 2022).

[234] My mother's family possessed the BRCA gene related breast cancer, which being autosomal dominant means almost half the women in each generation will develop breast cancer. I explore the scepter of BRCA-gene breast cancer in the narrative poem "She lived with the Knowledge" (Nisker J, *Ars Medica* 2004, 1(1), 75–80), and in the full-length play *Sarah's*

And after my residency I went to California
To do a research-fellowship in cancer prevention[235]
And Sid came down to San Francisco to visit
And shared a bedroom with of my eldest

It was many years later when I next saw Sid
Waiting for an elevator at Toronto General
I was there to give a seminar
And Sid was a staff radiologist there
This chance meeting and our long-hug greeting
Washed me in the warmth of our high school years
Sid walking to school with Mark[236] and me
Silently listening to our high school stories

Daughters (Nisker, *From Calcedonies to Orchids: Plays Promoting Humanity in Health Policy*, Iguana Press 2012).

[235] My research focused on prevention of estrogen-related cancers like breast cancer and endometrial cancer. However, I was unsuccessful in furthering prevention of breast cancer.

[236] See Chapter 9 "High School Best Friend Mark."

Chapter 18

Does a Teacher's Blip Flip After 50 Years of Marriage

In our gym's distant corner
A trampoline infringed on basketball practice
Especially when a girl in the year behind us
Did flips and half-twists upon it
A major distraction from practice
Though our coach insisted "Just ignore her"
But we still watched her because we adored her
So her trampoline was sentenced to "the dungeon"[237]

The gymnast was so elastic
She could twist her body into lovely knots
As if she was made of Silly Putty[238]

---

[237] "The dungeon" was a small dusty storage room off the gym, filled with ancient gym equipment.

[238] Silly Putty is a sort of clay advertised excessively on TV. One of its bonus attributes is that if you press it on inky comic book paper it can lift off the images.

Or the prettiest of plasticines
Allan[239] was so enamoured with the gymnast
He would watch her through the dungeon's door
That had to be kept open for ventilation
So our coach had to bench him

But after practice Allan would shower quickly
And wait for the gymnast on the sidewalk
Until her provocative practice was finished
And Allan would offer to walk her home
However the gymnast always refused him
As well as similar attempts by other students
Because her eyes were focused on the Olympics
And she didn't want to be distracted by a relationship

The gymnast's flips were under the supervision
Of a young Phys Ed teacher new to our school
Who all the guys liked for several reasons
In addition to his trim blonde wife
Who we would surreptitiously ogle
Whenever she came to practices and games
And she became a major distraction in the stands
But was never sentenced to the dungeon

The Phys Ed teacher was the energetic coach
Of our Junior basketball team when I was on it
Though he looked young enough to be one of the players
And we begged him to put on a uniform for tough games
But he also had to teach history
To complete his high school duties
And the girls competed to sit in the front seats
So they could be nearer their beloved teacher

---

[239] See Chapter 16 "Always Serious Allan."

However their beloved teacher was enamoured
With the fantastic-elastic gymnast
And he helped her accomplish her twists and flips
That insisted he touch her abdomen and legs
Albeit respectfully never sexually
And with the eyes of all of us watching
Feeling jealous because of what he was touching
Rather than seeing his touching as a problem

It wasn't till a rumour started spreading
That the teacher had left his lovely wife
And he and the gymnast had moved in together
That we appreciated the teacher's sin
First because of the power imbalance
That put the gymnast in a vulnerable position
Second because it was impossible for we students
To compete with a teacher for a girl's affection

Yet is it possible for us to reconsider
The nature of the teacher's sin
As he and the gymnast have been married
For more than a half-century[240]
Or perhaps we should not reconsider
For a sin is still a sin
Even if the sin leads to a happy ending
As the teacher-student relationship is sacred[241]

---

[240] This information, as usual, comes from Allan.

[241] A generation later a similar teacher-student relationship devastated my middle son's closest friend, when his long-term high school girlfriend entered a relationship with a different yet similar Phys Ed teacher.

Chapter 19

Mr. Kerr's Physics Antics

Mr. Kerr was our Senior physics teacher
And a creature beyond other teachers
In his outlandish classroom antics
That diminished our respect for physics
Such as throwing chalk at his students
For not paying attention or wrong-answering questions
And often with no apparent reason
So our physics texts were always ready to deflect

Mr. Kerr had been a Sergeant in World War II
And used military maneuvers in the classroom
Ordering us to stand at attention to answer questions
And remain at attention if the answer was incorrect
As well as addressing him crisply with "Sir"
Before and after we attempted an answer
Yet for some reason I liked Mr. Kerr's classes
Perhaps because I was enamoured with physics

And because he showed us Kodachrome of his cottage

Mr. Kerr built by himself on a Haliburton[242] lake
Without the help of a single nail
Just hundreds of hatcheted "dove-tails"
As Mr. Kerr clicked forward on his slide projector
He also took pride in the pine-forest slides
And smiled which was rare for Mr. Kerr
And I smiled because I also loved Haliburton[243]

Mr. Kerr returned exams like other teachers
In reverse order of the grade on the front page
However Mr. Kerr unlike other teachers
Returned low-mark papers with his foot
Dragging the papers along the floor's dirt
To illustrate what he thought the paper was worth
I considered this Kerr-antic his worst
And second guessed taking Physics in University

When Mr. Kerr returned my winter term exam
I noticed he had made an addition error
That when corrected would bestow ten marks more
So of course I brought the error to his attention
Mr. Kerr reluctantly re-added my exam
And even more reluctantly adjusted my mark
Then asked Erle[244] to return his exam paper
And added ten marks because "Erle's top brain"

I thought this Kerr-antic fantastic
Because Erle was a close friend
And hoped to stand "First" in the Province
And win the big scholarships that came with "First"
While I just hoped to win the next basketball game

---

[242] Haliburton is just south of Algonquin Park in Central Ontario, Canada.
[243] I was fortunate to attend summer camp in Haliburton, and in my '40s purchase a century-old log cabin there.
[244] See Chapter 7 "Brilliant Erle."

And most of my friends wished the same
And we applauded Erle standing "First" at graduation
And being handed the trophy by Mr. Kerr

I remember Mr. Kerr with some fondness
Albeit less fondness than other teachers
As Mr. Kerr's outrageous classroom antics
Were often more than inappropriate
Though I was never the brunt of Mr. Kerr's antics
Or for that matter any other teacher's antics
And actually looked forward to Mr. Kerr's classes
As they were the most unpredictable of high school classes

Chapter 20

Favourite Runnymede Cheerleader

Runnymede's cheerleaders were the sweetest
All blondes like their Swedish parents
Who had emigrated to Runnymede's neighbourhood
And the men worked in the enormous stockyards
Of which I had no knowledge
Till in a taxi on my first trip to Runnymede
When I sensed the stench of slaughter
Even before we were slaughtered on its claustrophobic court

Runnymede's head cheerleader seemed to be a Senior
And she was taller than the other cheerleaders
And her hair was so blonde it was almost white
And she was quite a delicious sight
I heard her being called Signe
Which I guess was something Swedish
Such as her name or perhaps our leader
But we didn't bring with a Swedish translator

Fifteen years later I saw Signe again

She had married her high school sweetheart Ken
Who by then was an obstetrician at Western[245]
And he would become one of my mentors and friends
Ken was a gentle giant
A gift to his staff and patients
At a time when arrogance was common in surgeons
With of course the exception of Dr. Allen[246]

When my rookieness dictated obsessive carefulness
Ken encouraged me onward with amazing patience
Even though his patience made him late for his next patient
Much to the chagrin of each anaesthetist
Ken's patience also made him late for dinner
However Signe accepted the importance of teaching
Going back to her years as a high school teacher
And even further to her Runnymede student years

When Signe and Ken moved to London
They settled on a farm a half-hour out of town
And Signe learned to be a farmer
While she was raising four children
As well as preparing dinners for her family
And more important for Ken's residents
While he delivered seminars on delivering children
And we were grateful to both of them

When Ken was suffering terminal cancer
I would visit my friend every evening after work
And Signe was always there caring for him
Whether in the hospital or on their farm
It seemed like Signe's strength was holding Ken together

---

[245] Western University in London, Canada.
[246] Dr. Hugh Allen was a famous cancer surgeon (See "I'm Sorry Vaccine Came Too Late for You Janet" *In* Nisker J., *Love and Injustice in Medicine*, Iguana Books, 2022).

She was still always smiling and reassuring
Though she knew her boyfriend was nearing his end
And Signe's courage supported all of Ken's friends

At the small lunch following Ken's funeral
Signe supported all of us as usual
Until she sensed tears behind my sunglasses
Then hugged me hard and whispered
"Jeff please help me keep it together
I promised not to cry but seeing you I can't help it
Because you and Ken and I go back such a long way
All the way to our high school days"

Chapter 21

Miss Hamilton's Periodic Table[247]

Miss Hamilton was our Senior chemistry teacher
The year before she decided to retire
Not that our chem-mischief encouraged her retirement
As Miss Hamilton was already a senior citizen
And we were quiet in Miss Hamilton's class
Perhaps because Miss Hamilton's voice was quiet
Or that she reminded us of our grandmothers
So being kind to her was almost assured

When Miss Hamilton chalked The Periodic Table on the blackboard
My eyes riveted on it in poetic wonder
And I still love The Periodic Table's logic
And still find myself contemplating its magic

---

[247] The Periodic Table is a chart of the elements organized according to their atomic number, starting with the lowest, hydrogen, and progressing to the new highest Oganesson. Many years after I sat in Miss Hamilton's class, I read Primo Levi's brilliant novel, *The Periodic Table*, describing his survival in Auschwitz-Birkenau because the Nazis thought his knowledge of chemistry might be useful (Levi P., *The Periodic Table*, translated by Raymond Rosenthal, Penguin Classics, 2000).

Especially while I'm running or swimming
Or paddling on a gentle stream
Listening to Miss Hamilton quietly breathing
The Periodic Table into my being

Miss Hamilton was the epitome of a dedicated teacher
But her chemistry labs were more than boring
So we made things more exciting by having snowball fights
With the Styrofoam nuclei of the molecules we were building[248]
Of course we tried not to hit Miss Hamilton
But when the intensity of snowball throws increased
Some snowballs rebounded off the blackboard
And hit Miss Hamilton on the back of her head[249]

But more often they only hit Miss Hamilton's back
And she knew these hits were unintended
So they didn't distract her from her teaching
And again we weren't the reason Miss Hamilton retired
The snowball fights had to stop when she had us surround
Each Styrofoam nucleus with Styrofoam electrons
That we plugged into the nucleus with knitting needles
Making further snowball fights potentially lethal

However Senior Chem had serious problems
That weren't at all Miss Hamilton's fault
The first was the toluene-blue we put into test tubes
Before the centrifuge and scintillation counter
The second was the chemical benzene
Whose ring looked elegant on the blackboard
But seemed dizzily toxic to us

---

[248] We used our chemistry texts as snowball shields like we did with garbage-can lids in winter.
[249] We never threw snowballs when she was chalking the blackboard because rebounds would hit her in the face.

But not even Miss Hamilton knew how toxic[250]

I thought of Miss Hamilton frequently
During my Post-Doc in Biochemistry
But never developed her love for the subject
Though California was a great place to study it
Under the tutelage of a famous "Finn"[251]
Who didn't like me as much as Miss Hamilton did
Because I wanted to be a clinician not a chemist
And I wanted to be a teacher like Miss Hamilton

Miss Hamilton is still alive as I write this
I know this from Mr. Perkins[252] rather than Allan[253]
And I'm sure Miss Hamilton is over a hundred
And I'm glad the chemicals didn't do her in
Not even the toluene or benzene
Both of which have since been proven carcinogenic[254]
And thus no longer used in high schools
In Chemistry classes like Miss Hamilton's

---

[250] Benzene pollution from chemical factories in Sarnia, Ontario, less than an hour from our hospital, continues to cause health problems for the Aamjiwnaang First Nation (Becken B., "Aamjiwnaang First Nation members say industrial benzene emissions in Sarnia, Ont. area made them ill," *CBC News*, Apr 18, 2024).

[251] Professor Penti Siiteri preferred to be called "Finn."

[252] See Chapter 4 "Favourite Teacher Mr. Perkins."

[253] See Chapter 16 "Always Serious Allan."

[254] Dees C, Askari M, Henley D. "Carcinogenic potential of benzene and toluene when evaluated using cyclin-dependent kinase activation and p53-DNA binding." *Environ Health Perspect.* 1996 Dec;104 Suppl 6(Suppl 6):1289-92. doi: 10.1289/ehp.961041289. PMID: 9118908; PMCID: PMC1469723).

Chapter 22

Sharpie Jackie

Jackie was the smallest of us
Thus the favourite target of the class bully
Thus I often had to step in to defend Jackie
And earned the moniker "Jackie-lover"
However Jackie was sharper than the rest of us
Perhaps inheriting his business sense from his father
Though none of us were sure of his father's work
But we sure liked his little blonde mother

She gave Jackie her ancient Ford Meteor
Which was a two-door in an odd brownish colour
And was the cheapest car on the market
Before the plethora of foreign cars invaded
I remember almost flying out the Meteor's passenger door
During one of Sharpie Jackie's too-sharp turns
And grabbing the armrest with all I had
Dragging last season's "Black Chucks"[255] along the asphalt

---

[255] See Chapter 6 "Black Chucks."

So Jackie tied the Meteor's door shut with old twine
From the steering wheel's stem to that armrest
And then to get in we had to slither under the steering wheel
Or tumbled through a window
But the armrest kept falling off
And Krazy Glue hadn't been invented yet
However the Meteor beat walking in winter till Senior Year
When my uncle gave me his equally-ancient Chevrolet Biscayne[256]

Sharpie Jackie played trombone in Mr. Perkins's[257] orchestra
Though it looked more like the trombone was playing him
Because Sharpie Jackie sharply jerked the slide
Instead of sliding it smoothly as Mr. Perkins repeatedly advised
Though I can only verify this Jackie machination
In the "pauses" indicating Mark[258] and I stop playing
On the sheet music Mr. Perkins[259] distributed
But told us to look at him not the music

Jackie's sharpness was demonstrated Senior Year
When the Vice bought new lockers for the Boys Locker Room[260]
And planned to have a scrap metal firm pick up the old ones
But Jackie volunteered to take the lockers off his hands
The Vice agreed and Jackie eagerly arranged
To sell the old lockers to a religious school

---

[256] The Chevrolet Biscayne competed with the Meteor for being least-expensive North American car. After two years in my possession, the Biscayne's motor caught on fire at my favourite make out spot on the Scarborough bluffs overlooking Lake Ontario, as it was winter so we had to keep its motor running. I told my date that the fire was caused by sparks from our electric kissing. Thinking about in-car kissing reminds me of the song "Paradise By the Dashboard Light" (Meat Loaf 1977).
[257] See Chapter 4 "Favourite Teacher Mr. Perkins."
[258] See Chapter 9 "High School Best Friend Mark."
[259] See Chapter 4 "Favourite Teacher Mr. Perkins."
[260] See "Preface."

That didn't have funds to purchase new lockers
Thus had to accept the kick-dents on ours[261]

And every spring during hockey playoffs
Jackie always had at least one "pool" going
And none of us thought buying his tickets was gambling
As after all hockey was our national sport
Jackie boldly posted the latest scores
On the bulletin board outside the cafeteria[262]
Along with a list of each pool's winners
But never mentioned the percentage he took

Jackie took abuse for his profits from this scheme
As well as for his other business dealings
And thought being a business lawyer appealing
But studying to get into law less appealing
As studying interfered with Jackie's business dealings
So Jackie became some sort of accountant instead
Thus his businesses could be seen as legitimate
At least by those who were in them with him

Jackie seems to have disappeared
Although I'm sure Allan[263] could track him down
And he might begin by excavating Bay St.[264]
Or even Wall St.[265] to find him
Or investigating who runs our Canadian lotteries
That may have been inspired by Jackie's high school pools
And Jackie would be happy to take a commission
If one of his ticket purchasers had a million-dollar win

---

[261] See "Preface."
[262] See Chapter 8 "Rag Doll."
[263] See Chapter 16 "Always Serious Allan."
[264] Bay St. in Toronto is the business capital of Canada.
[265] Wall St. in New York is the business capital of the United States.

Chapter 23

Mr. Petrecek Favourite Czech French Teacher

Mr. Petrecek was our French teacher
Even though he was Czechoslovakian
And spoke with a strong Czechoslovakian accent
Like Victor Laszlo's in Casablanca[266]
Mr. Petrecek's enthusiasm was infectious
Even though he taught us our least favourite subject
And he was an incredibly animated teacher
Almost as animated as Mr. Perkins[267]

---

[266] *Casablanca* (1942), directed by Michael Curtiz, is my favourite film. Victor Laszlo, portrayed by Paul Henreid, is the Czechoslovakian resistance leader who boards the airplane to Lisbon at the end of the film to continue his fight against the Nazis. Humphrey Bogart as Rick, encouraged Victor Laszlo's wife, Ilsa, portrayed by Ingrid Bergman, to get on the plane with her husband to support him "in his work," even though Rick and Ilsa were in love.

[267] Mr. Perkins taught us Music (See Chapter 4 "Favourite Teacher Mr. Perkins").

But some of the guys found Mr. Petrecek humourous
And laughed when he was being serious
Even the girls who afforded teachers more respect
Often laughed at Mr. Petrecek

And joined in teasing Mr. Petrecek
Though he was obviously a good guy
And it wasn't his fault he was given the awful task
Of trying to teach us our least-favourite subject

Mr. Petrecek attempted to be liked by his students
Even when we weren't being nice to him
And I have to admit to being guilty
Of initiating a few pranks on him
For example Mr. Petrecek sat us in alphabetical order
Which put me in the front seat of row three
Conveniently close to his briefcase
Being ignored on the floor beside it

So his briefcase had a tendency to wander
Between the desks of row two and three
With assistance from row two and three students
Before hiding behind the legs of the other Jeff
Where Mr. Petrecek's briefcase would remain hidden
Even after French class had finished
When Mr. Petrecek started searching for his briefcase
Which upset him every day[268]

Another prank I instigated was prompted
By the manner in which Mr. Petrecek dismissed the class
Making us wait in our seats till he said "Allez allez"
Long after the bell's drilling had faded away

---

[268] We never suspected personal items might be in Mr. Petrecek's briefcase, and of course never opened it. That would have been too rude even for us.

Then he would mischievously look at us
Even opening his mouth to fake "Allez allez"
Then smile and stare at the ceiling for a minute
While we were all eager to get going to Music[269]

But sometimes when he would finally say "Allez allez"
My classmates stayed fixed in their seats
Until I stood up and said "Allez allez"
And we laughingly got on our way
Hearing a distraught Mr. Petrecek shouting
"Who is the boss here who is the boss here"
So my exiting classmates pointed at me
As we left Mr. Petrecek's class quickly[270]

Far more important than being our French teacher
Mr. Petrecek started a boys volleyball team
Building on his experience of playing
On the Czechoslovakian National Team
And Mr. Petrecek had the inspired idea
That basketball players could be taught volleyball
And asked me to ask my basketball teammates
If they wanted to play volleyball in the fall[271]

Some of the guys thought "Why not"
Even though we considered volleyball a girly sport
But as Men's Volleyball had just entered the Olympics[272]
We had to admit that it was legitimate
And Mr. Petrecek's enthusiasm was so infectious
We started taking volleyball seriously

---

[269] See Chapter 4 "Favourite Teacher Mr. Perkins."
[270] I must admit I did feel guilty for harassing this pleasant man, but not enough to limit my pranks.
[271] Basketball season didn't start till after Christmas.
[272] Men's volleyball made its Olympic debut at the 1964 Games in Tokyo just before I started high school.

And the more seriously we took it the better we became
And found ourselves in the City Championship game

In fact volleyball was the only team I played on
That actually made it to the City Finals
But East York also made it to the Finals
So we didn't progress to the Provincials
Just because East York had one exceptional player
Who was six four and muscled all over[273]
And his serve was unanswerable
Whether we tried to block it at the net or dig it off the floor

Mr. Petrecek started Saul[274] and Mark[275] and I in the front row
Putting our best digger Larry in back centre[276]
But this guy's serves came so hard with so much top-spin[277]
That even Larry could rarely "bump" it
When he did I would try to hit it higher
Hoping it would wind up in the wheelhouse of Saul[278]
But we just couldn't return this guy's serve
So the Finals were over before they started

I find it interesting to recall
That our only team to make the finals was in volleyball
A sport we only started playing in Senior Year
And our team was small for volleyball except for Saul[279]
So our success rests on the shoulders of Mr. Petrecek

---

[273] This student was already playing on the provincial team and would soon play on the national team.
[274] See Chapter 24 "Tall Saul."
[275] See Chapter 9 "High School Best Friend Mark."
[276] There are six players on each team, loosely aligned in two rows for each serve.
[277] Top-spin allows the ball to go higher over the net to avoid blockers then dip to hit the court.
[278] See Chapter 24 "Tall Saul."
[279] See Chapter 24 "Tall Saul."

Who taught us well his Olympic sport
And we preferred his teaching us volleyball
Over his teaching us French of course

Chapter 24

Tall Saul

Saul was the tallest of us
Saul lived near Erle[280] and Gillda[281]
With his house backing on a "green space"
And a beautiful wildflower field
Before they were dug up for a subway tunnel[282]
But at least this "subway" would be covered in green
Not rocketing ferociously above ground
Like it could be seen beside Sam's house[283]

Saul's sister Raisa was a year ahead of us
And a genius of almost Erle's[284] calibre

---

[280] See Chapter 7 "Brilliant Erle."
[281] See Chapter 28 "Gillda and Sam."
[282] The Spadina subway ran from the north end of Toronto along the Spadina (now Allen) Expressway above ground, before it went mostly underground from Saul's house to downtown.
[283] See Chapter 28 "Gillda and Sam."
[284] See Chapter 7 "Brilliant Erle."

And received a full scholarship to MIT[285]
To study theoretical mathematics
But she wasn't tall like Saul
And didn't play girls basketball
Though I now see her commenting on TV frequently
And she recently came to a seminar I gave at U of T[286]

Tall Saul was naturally our team's centre
But his slender frame let him get pushed around
By the bulkier centres of other teams
Especially when positioning for rebounds
Indeed Saul took a pounding
But he was brave and never complained
So we kept "feeding" him beneath the basket
Bounce-passing the ball through "the key"

We all had a fondness for Saul
Because he was brave and a good guy
And always gave his everything
Which meant everything to his teammates
However we cringed the day after games
When we took in Saul's blackened eyes
And saw him holding his bruised ribs
Repeatedly taped by our school's nurse

We were all proud of Tall Saul
Of his courage and tenacity
And his never complaining in the locker room after games
Even after we played George Harvey[287]
Yet I haven't seen Saul since high school
When he left Toronto to go to Kingston

---

[285] Massachusetts Institute of Technology.
[286] University of Toronto.
[287] George Harvey was the technical school in our district. George Harvey's centre outweighed Saul by at least fifty pounds and had vicious elbows.

To study civil engineering at Queens
So he could make everything green[288]

---

[288] Saul's high-school experience of watching the destruction of the green space behind his home may have contributed to his civil engineering specialization in restoration, and his company being called Greening Homes (https://greeninghomes.com/).

Chapter 25

Toronto's First OXFAM March

In my final year of high school
Toronto held its initial OXFAM[289] March
As the starving children in Biafra[290]
Began receiving TV attention
Our Vice agreed we should participate
And gave me the honour of organizing this
Which I eagerly did as a march for hungry children in Africa
Is a march for hungry children everywhere[291]

Students from all high schools were encouraged to gather
In a park east of the start of the Gardiner[292]
And march to City Hall together

---

[289] Oxford Committee for Famine Relief.
[290] Starvation in Biafra was caused by famine compounded by the Nigerian Civil War (1967 to 1970). We were sickened by television images of the swollen abdomens of starving Biafran children.
[291] Including Canada.
[292] The Gardiner Expressway runs across Toronto along Lake Ontario.

But getting to that park would be hard for our students[293]
So I thought it better to meet at our school
Then march to City Hall as a solitary unit
And was ecstatic when I arrived at school at eight
And saw hundreds of students ready to participate

They were overflowing the street near the front entrance
Cheering "Colours red and blue and gold"
It was my proudest moment in high school
And moisture accumulated behind my sunglasses
I had asked the Senior Band to lead our marchers
The twenty kilometres to City Hall
And the cacophony meant that at least half the band's members
Were already there warming up their instruments

We had never been a "marching band" before
Thus we didn't have portable music or instrument clips
So some of the band duct-taped crib sheets
To the back of the musician in front of them
This worked for the woodwinds and trumpets
But less so for the slide trombones
So Marabeth[294] suggested we keep the music basic
Just our school song over and over[295]

There was harmony in us playing together
In support of children in Biafra
And harmony in our new school spirit
That lasted the rest of Senior Year

---

[293] It would have taken well over an hour of bus, streetcar, subway, and another streetcar, followed by a long walk even before the march started.
[294] See Chapter 11 "Marabeth the Best of Us."
[295] At one point we tried to improvise "Louie Louie" (The Kingsmen, 1963), but it was a disaster.

As if we could still hear our drummer[296]
Steadily beating our hearts together
Poetically giving us united purpose
With every step forward we took

At each stoplight I turned around
And basked in the bath of our hundreds of students
Taking action on an early Saturday morning
When they could have been peacefully sleeping in
And when we spotted City Hall's curves in the distance
A great enthusiasm swept over us
And we spontaneously chanted our school song
Rather than playing it on our instruments

When we entered Nathan Phillips Square[297]
We were welcomed by banners and flags
As well as the many students who had walked in the main group
Along the much shorter Gardiner route
And a new energy infused us when we discovered
No other school did the march as one unit
Even the Mayor[298] came down to the Square to greet us
Amazed we marched all the way from our school together

I reminisce this first OXFAM March
Whenever I see a TV request for OXFAM donations
A half-century since our first OXFAM March
A half-century of more starving children
Our OXFAM March is but another gift
Generously bestowed on me in high school

---

[296] Our drummer duct-taped two leather belts to his snare drum to serve as a drum-carrier.
[297] Nathan Phillips Square is the cement area in front of City Hall, named for the mayor who had supported City Hall's modern design. In winter the area becomes a popular skating rink.
[298] William Dennison was Toronto's mayor from 1967 to 1972.

A gift I continue to try to share
With hungry children in Canada[299]

---

[299] Rev Susan Eagle set up soup kitchens in London, and included me on the Board of Directors as her "White male spokesman" at City Hall.

Chapter 26

The Prom

The most "formal" of our high school dances
Was of course our annual Prom
Always held at Casa Loma
An enormous medieval castle[300]
Perched large on the precipice
Of a glacier-carved cliff
With parapets standing guard over downtown Toronto
And Lake Ontario beyond[301]

The castle is replete with formal gardens
Riding stables and greenhouses
Carpentry workshops and pottery wheels
Now resources for Toronto's people
Including the many high school students

---

[300] The castle was built by Sir Henry Pellatt from 1911 to 1914 (https://casaloma.ca/).
[301] The glacier's melt created Lake Algonquin, which receded over what is now downtown Toronto, and partially remains as Lake Ontario (Fyon A. (2017) https://www.ontariobeneathourfeet.com/glacial-lake-algonquin).

Who dress up for their Prom in the castle's ballroom
Many of whom will a few years later
Dress up for their wedding in the castle's atrium[302]

I always looked forward to our Prom[303]
Except for the consternation the month before
Regarding who would be my Prom date
As I never seemed to be "going steady"
Neither were any of my friends
With the exception of Gillda and Sam[304]
Thus who would be one's Prom date
Was an important high school question

As being asked to be one's Prom date meant something
Especially if it was the right person doing the asking
And if it wasn't it was promblematic
Because your Prom date set your standard
Thus your potential Prom date was effused with the hope
That your hoped-for Prom date would see you as a Prom date
And just to be safe both ways
My non-girlfriend Gail[305] and I were always Prom dates

There were other aspects of our Prom
That this late-60s teen thought promblematic
Including the election of the Prom Queen[306]
And her entourage of six Princesses
There was something wrong with this long tradition
As it reinforced importance of physical beauty

---

[302] I was last at Casa Loma for the wedding of a medical student.
[303] Because I loved dancing (See Chapter 2 "Friday Night Dances"), though I loathed dressing up.
[304] See Chapter 28 "Gillda and Sam."
[305] See Chapter 15 "The Girl Everyone Thought I Would Marry."
[306] See Chapter 27 "Queen Tamarra."

Yet my social-conscious non-girlfriend Gail[307]
Was ecstatic to be chosen as a Princess

The Prom was even more promblematic
In that the dress code called for "formal"
Forcing the guys to rent a "monkey-suit"
Which I of course refused to do
For the expense of renting "formal wear"
Was prohibitive in a high school like ours
Where most students were immigrants[308] or their children
With no extra money for such nonsense

And the girls were expected to wear a gown
Which meant hours of excavating used-clothing stores
Or succumbing to gown-rental stores
Or labouring over a sewing machine[309]
So when I was finally in Senior Year
And had a bit of influence on Students Council[310]
I campaigned for a change in dress code
And our Prom became "semi-formal"

The guys could wear a jacket and tie
Though dress pants were still required
Above our Italian shoes[311] that could slide smooth
Over Casa Loma's parquet-wood floor
More important "semi-formal" permitted

---

[307] See Chapter 15 "The Girl Everyone Thought I Would Marry."
[308] See Chapter 5 "Friendly Salvatore."
[309] Gail had to sew her own gown because she was too tall for the gowns at the used-clothing and gown-rental stores (See Chapter 15 "The Girl Everyone Thought I Would Marry"). In our high school yearbook there is a picture of Gail in her home-sewn gown, smiling beside the other princesses, and Tamarra our Prom Queen (See Chapter 27 "Queen Tamarra").
[310] I was the "Athletic Association Delegate."
[311] Impeached American President Nixon speaks of admiration for Italian shoes in Oliver Stone's film *Nixon* (1995).

The girls to wear miniskirts
Making dancing more fun for them
Not to mention for their friends

But a Prom problem I couldn't mend
Was the expense of the obligatory corsage
A waste of money at any cost
But when I campaigned against corsages I lost
I remember entering a flower shop
To purchase a corsage for Gail
And being blown away by the of cost of a single flower
Flimsily glued to an elastic wrist band

Another Prom problem I couldn't mend
Was the long tradition of renting a limo
Again something wrong with this frivolous expense
As it further promoted difference among students
Many of whom were already struggling with
Prom tickets and corsages and "formal wear"
So even the thought of renting a limo
Was more than this late-60s teenager could bear

However in Senior Year I must confess
Several friends and I hypocritically rented a limo
To pick us up from "Fran's Restaurant"
Where we were going for Prom dinner first
Fran's was a casual diner on St. Clair
And as its patrons stared at our formal wear
And we felt even more uncomfortable after dinner
Being chauffeured in a limo[312] to Casa Loma

---

[312] I was even more uncomfortable in a limo in my late-40s, when our physician rock band, Bold Fingers, was asked to play a fundraiser at the Royal Ontario Museum in Toronto. The organizers of this event for 1,500 donors advertised us as a famous rock band from the States, and were using the limo as a trope to further their narrative.

As I reflect back on our Prom
I saw it as a major high school Promblem
Yet I participated in much of the regalia
Except for the monkey-suit of course
My participation speaks of being more of a conformist
Than this late-60s teenager wanted to be
Constantly railing against inequity and inequality
But was too enamoured with high school to always be

Chapter 27

Queen Tamarra

Tamarra was a beautiful goddess
Too beautiful to be looked at by mortals like us
Let alone smiled at though I timidly tried
And Tamarra would graciously smile back
In January of our Senior Year
Tamarra was elected Prom Queen
And she was the most beautiful Prom Queen ever
In the history of our high school or any other

Yet Tamarra was far from being full of herself
Never appearing superior or standoffish
Rather Tamarra was always warm and friendly
Though I kept my distance for fear of blushing
As prior to eye-witnessing Tamarra
I couldn't imagine a girl being too beautiful
Yet Tamarra's beauty was disturbing to me
For reasons remaining a mystery for a half-century

Of course all the guys had a crush on Tamarra

Even though she was too far above us for crushes
But she would smile at each of us as if she was equal to us
Because of the modesty Tamarra possessed
None of that look-at-me-I'm-beautiful image
Girls with Tamarra's visage could possess
Rather Tamarra tried hard to be the same as us
But her blonde beauty subverted equality

Tamarra had a boyfriend or bodyguard
Who looked more than ten years older than us
When he dropped Tamarra off at school each morning
And picked her up as soon as classes ended
And glared menacingly if I dared to look at him
And even more menacingly if I dared to look at Tamarra
And his eyes' daggers were switchblade sharp
And rumour had it he had a gun

Tamarra left high school before graduation
To work full-time as a model at Eaton's
Where she walked runways displaying fashions
Wealthy women would buy to look like Tamarra[313]
Allan[314] once showed me a picture of Tamarra
Smiling from an Eaton's ad in the Toronto Star[315]
Not looking superior like the other three models
Who weren't even close to being as beautiful as Tamarra

Ten years after high school graduation
Tamarra smiled at me from the front cover
Of the "Eaton's Christmas Catalogue" at our door
And I just smiled back at her in wonder

---

[313] Eaton's fashion shows and luncheons for wealthy women were held at its upscale Eaton's College St. store (See Chapter 13 "York Memo Girl").
[314] See Chapter 16 "Always Serious Allan."
[315] The *Toronto Star* was Canada's largest circulation newspaper (See Chapter 14 "Solid Paul").

For even on the famous catalogue's cover
Tamarra smiled modestly with no officiousness
As if being on the cover of "Eaton's Christmas Catalogue"
Meant nothing to Tamarra but another job

Tamarra's smile had no expiration date
Nor did her eye's twinkle diminish in grace
Nor did the way Tamarra's quiet joy embraced
All of us brave enough to gaze her way
Tamarra's no expiration date continues to this day
As while writing her poem I excavated my final yearbook
And there was Tamarra smiling from its glossy pages
With the Prom Queen crown on her head

Tamarra's eyes still magnetically engaged me
As did her still glimmering smile
And her picture still conveyed a modest presence
Even with a glittering crown on her head
I hadn't thought about Tamarra for a half-century
But in writing her poem she came back vividly
For Tamarra will always be my Prom Queen
Although I'm sure she has no memory of me

Chapter 28

Gillda and Sam

Gillda could have stood second to Erle[316] in high school
Like she stood second to Erle in elementary school
But she met Sam[317] at our first Friday Night Dance[318]
And began standing first in her long love for him
And on that enchanted evening[319]
Gillda and Sam were electro-magnetically attracted
Just like Tony and Maria in *West Side Story*[320]

---

[316] See Chapter 7 "Brilliant Erle."

[317] I write about Sam and how his death extended my life in "But All You Need is a Good Index Finger" *In* Nisker J., *Love and Injustice in Medicine*, Iguana Books, 2022.

[318] See Chapter 2 "Friday Night Dances."

[319] "Some Enchanted Evening" (1949) is a love song from Rodgers and Hammerstein's "South Pacific."

[320] *West Side Story* is a Broadway musical brilliantly composed by Leonard Berstein, with lyrics by Stephen Sondheim, choreography by Jerome Robbins, and book by Arthur Laurents. The 1961 film version, directed by Robert Wise and Jerome Robbins, won ten Academy Awards including "Best Motion Picture" (https://awardsdatabase.oscars.org/search/results). The more recent film version in 2021, directed by Steven Spielberg, with screenplay by Tony Kushner won seven Academy Awards.

In a remarkably similar gym-dance scene

Gillda took German as her elective
Rather than music like Sam and the rest of us
Which put Gillda in all different classes[321]
So they looked forward to lunch hour to see each other[322]
Sam played viola in Mr. Perkins's orchestra[323]
But not as well Marabeth's[324] father in the Toronto Symphony
And I'm not sure if Sam's bow was just another cat-tormentor
As the four clarinets were at the back with the brass

Otherwise Sam sat beside me through high school
Then through Pre Meds and Meds
At least in the few lectures we attended
And Sam was my lab partner and clinic partner
And also my assignment partner and carpool partner
And ILLEGAL PARKING ticket partner
And cadaver-formaldehyde partner
And we felt naked when not next to each other

At the end of third year Med School
Gillda and Sam were the first to "tie the knot"
And their small reception was at Casa Loma
Where we had gone to our Proms together[325]
And the sparkling evening weather
Forecast a brilliant future for them together
Until Sam's cancer tore them apart
No matter how lovingly Gillda sutured Sam's heart

---

[321] In our high school the composition of classes in all subjects was based on our one elective.
[322] See Chapter 3 "Frank and Suzy."
[323] See Chapter 4 "Favourite Teacher Mr. Perkins."
[324] See Chapter 11 "Marabeth the Best of Us."
[325] See Chapter 26 "The Prom."

The last time I saw Gillda and Sam
Sam was in a semi-comatose condition
In the bedroom Gillda made for him off their kitchen
When Sam was perforated with metastatic cancer[326]
I hugged Sam and silently wept
Holding back tears at Gillda's behest
There was nothing I could do for Sam
Though I stupidly told Gillda "I have an oncologist friend"

Gillda led me back into the kitchen
Where I watched her stir Sam's chicken soup medicine[327]
Hoping the love she was stirring in the soup
Would bring Sam back to her again
But I needed to be with Sam
And went back to his bed and clutched his upper left arm
For over an hour without his knowing it
And when I returned to the kitchen Gillda was still stirring

I asked Gillda if there was anything I could do for her
Knowing there would never be anything I could do for Sam
But Gillda just kept silently stirring
In a trance from which she didn't want to awaken
For the love of her life was being taken
And her companion for fifty years was being taken
And her plan for the future was being taken
And her desire to keep living was being taken

---

[326] Sam's death from metastatic prostate cancer prompted me to have a PSA test, which I had previously refused because it wasn't yet publicly funded (See "The Arrogance of 'But All You Need Is a Good Index Finger'" *In* Nisker J. *Love and Injustice in Medicine*, Iguana Books, 2022). The social justice me needed to walk my talk that insisted public funding should be provided for all cancer screening. My PSA test was positive, and my bone scan revealed metastatic lesions up my spine just like Sam's bone scan. I would be dead if not for Sam.

[327] Chicken soup is "medicine" in the Jewish tradition, and probably works a bit by "pushing fluids."

I kept watching Gillda stir Sam's chicken soup medicine
For what seemed an hour but was probably less
When my emerging tears insisted I exit
Before they further submerged Gillda
At the door I hugged a rigid Gillda
Then scribbled phone numbers on Sam's prescription pad
And offered to return to Toronto at a moment's notice
If there was anything I could ever do for her

On my two hour drive back to London
I mourned the imminent loss of my dearest friend
And as raindrops cluttered the windshield
I wiped them off with my left hand
But finally decided to pull off the highway
So I could sob freely without causing an accident
I needed to be with Sam again
And could not accept I would never see him again

Sam's smiling picture sits on my office desk
And Sam caresses me from his picture
Every morning as I walk in my office
Every morning as I miss Sam
It is not fair that the kindest of us
Have to be the first to leave us[328]
But that's the injustice of medicine
And perhaps the injustice of love[329]

---

[328] The second was Wendy (See Chapter 14 "Solid Paul").
[329] Nisker J. *Love and Injustice in Medicine*, Iguana Books, 2022.

Chapter 29

John's Microbus

John was two years ahead of us in high school
And we thought him "real cool" because of his "wheels"
An orange Volkswagen Microbus[330]
With a creamy-white roof beneath the dust[331]
The engine was in the rear like in all Volkswagens
And struggled hard to propel the Microbus
As it was under-powered being the same engine
That even struggled to propel the Beetle[332]

The Microbus had three rows of hard seats
That could sit six people albeit uncomfortably
And a seventh could be squeezed in on the floor
Between the middle row and sliding side door
You could only sit two in the front

---

[330] In 2025 Volkswagen introduced a new lithium-ion-battery version of the Microbus called the "Buzz."
[331] The direct route to high school included a dusty unpaved road.
[332] The Volkswagen Beetle was one of the smallest cars in my high school years, and seemed even smaller because most of the cars were enormous.

Because the Microbus had a dangerous stick shift
That vibrated viscously at stop signs
And just a bit less when the engine whined[333]

John was almost as tall as Saul[334]
However John played piano not basketball
And attempted to teach me in my home
Where we had a piano that no one could play[335]
But my father said "There's something wrong with John"
And didn't want him in our home
Even though John was teaching me piano
A gift for which I will always be beholden

John lived next door to Sid[336]
In a modern open-concept home
So the grand piano in John's living room
Could be seen through all first-floor windows
Some mornings John would pick us up in his Microbus
And ferry us the rest of the kilometres to school
And some evenings show up after practice
Just to give us a lift home in the dark

One day John said he was learning college wrestling
And wanted to practice his moves on me
Though he seemed to prefer being "taken down"[337]
And staying pinned when my move was finished
We wrestled on a thick carpet in our basement

---

[333] John taught me to drive "standard" with this stick shift.

[334] See Chapter 24 "Tall Saul."

[335] We had a small Mason & Risch upright piano in our living room for decorative purposes.

[336] See Chapter 17 "Quiet Sid."

[337] "A takedown" occurs when a wrestler flattens his opponent on the mat. The wrestler receives several points for a "takedown" (https://www.ncaa.com/news/wrestling/article/2020-09-16/how-college-wrestling-match-scored).

That worked quite well as a wrestling mat
Yet wrestling increased my father's hate for John
And his repeating "There's something wrong with John"

John went to U of T[338] two years ahead of us
But still showed up after practice to give us a lift home
We just thought John was friendly and generous
And never thought there was "something wrong with John"
In Grade 12 Mark[339] and I were cruising Yorkville[340]
As per usual on a summer Saturday evening
When we spotted John being pounded by two guys
So of course we stopped to rip the guys off of him

It seemed John was often taking a beating
As seen in his often blackened eyes
And his holding his ribs when walking
Which made no sense as John was gentle and kind
And would never instigate a fight
Unlike many of the guys in our high school
Who liked to fight to display their aggressiveness
They thought required to assert their manliness

In May of my final year of high school
John flew off of the Bloor Street Viaduct
Onto the Don Valley Parkway far below
Where his body was crushed further by a truck
The Bloor Street Viaduct was originally famous

---

[338] University of Toronto.
[339] See Chapter 9 "High School Best Friend Mark."
[340] Music drifted through the open doors of many coffee houses in Yorkville so you never needed a ticket to hear Joni Mitchell or Gord Lightfoot. The street was so thronged with people that our car had to cruise slowly, which was a good thing as we took in the girls with naked middles above their jeans, or wearing almost-see-through "peasant dresses."

For bringing water to Toronto through its huge tubes[341]
But by the time I was in high school the Viaduct was infamous
For the many suicides off its bridge

There were no safety screens inhibiting jumping then[342]
So the Viaduct was a convenient site for suicide[343]
And John's body was just one more of the bodies
Found crushed below on the DVP
Supposedly John had been on a bad LSD trip
But one of my cousins insists John was pushed
Because John was pushing drugs and a deal had gone wrong
However I don't believe my cousin's version

I was a pallbearer at John's funeral
Defying the strong objections of my father
Who didn't want to see his son's picture in the Toronto Star
Closely associated with a drug dealer
But I accepted the pallbearer honour
As it was bestowed on me by John's mother
Who had just lost her only child
And I wasn't going to deny her

The Funeral Director led me to the front-left handle
Of John's long black-steel coffin
And I remember straining hard to lift it
Along with seven of John's neighbours

---

[341] The Bloor St. Viaduct was constructed between 1915 and 1919. Michael Ondaatje describes the building of the Viaduct in his 1987 novel *In the Skin of a Lion.*
[342] A 20-foot high curved-inward barbed-wire fence would be constructed to inhibit deaths like John's.
[343] When my grandmother was dying of metastatic breast cancer in her late 40s, my father would drive her across the Viaduct every morning to the old Princess Margaret Hospital for chemotherapy. Every morning my grandmother would beg him to throw her off the Viaduct's bridge because of the inconvenience she was causing him.

Indeed I was shocked by the coffin's heaviness
Compared with my grandmother's pine box
And the coffins of several of my cousins
In the generation before ours

During third year Med School I thought of John
Each time I drove across the Viaduct to Princess Margaret[344]
And I continue to think of John today
Whenever I try to play the piano
But most often I think of John
Whenever I see a Microbus
Either puttering on the street
Or in hippie-centred movies[345]

Thinking back on John today
It is possible that John was gay
Not that that mattered to me in any way
But may explain my father's hate
And the many beatings John would take
For reasons beyond explanation
But gay-hate was rampant in my high school days[346]
As gay-hate remains rampant to this day

---

[344] Princess Margaret Hospital was the cancer centre (See "Princess Margaret" *In* Nisker J. *Love and Injustice in Medicine*, Iguana Books, 2022).

[345] Like *Field of Dreams* (1989) directed by Phil Alden Robinson, starring Kevin Costner and James Earl Jones.

[346] When I was a summer-camper my weight-lifting macho counsellor would put on his black-leather jacket after lights out, telling us he was "going gay hunting in Orillia." Several counsellors went as a pack to attack supposedly gay men in Couchiching Beach Park near the statue of Samuel de Champlain.

Chapter 30

Eleanor's Legs

In Senior Year our class was immersed
With students who hadn't taken music[347]
Most important were the girls in "Commercial"
The most beautiful of whom was Eleanor
Eleanor came from Ireland and was a bit older
And still had an Irish lilt in her voice
But of which made Eleanor all the more attractive
To us born in Canada or in Italy[348] kids

While other guys were fixated on breasts
I was definitely a "legs man"
As brought to my attention by my friends
And Eleanor had the best legs
Easily observed below the shortest of miniskirts
That made her never-ending legs more prominent

---

[347] Until Senior Year the composition of all academic classes was based on our one elective.
[348] Many students in our high school were born in Italy (See Chapter 5 "Friendly Salvatore").

Accentuated by the sheerest of clear nylons
And I clearly had a crush on this woman

Eleanor like other girls who wore miniskirts
Had to pull her skirt down every time she stood
To answer certain teachers' questions
Or walk up to chalk the blackboard
And just as miniskirtedly-important
Eleanor had to pull her skirt down as she sat down
While we guys tried to avert our eyes
From Eleanor's variety of pastel-coloured underwear

Eleanor's legs became most prominent
When our perhaps lecherous English teacher
Got it in his head that learning Shakespeare was better
If we pushed our desks into a circle
I can't be sure whether our teacher knew for certain
He was putting Eleanor in a compromised position
Not to mention distracting almost-men from King Lear
Because even with turned heads Eleanor's long legs appeared

We all felt discomfort for Eleanor
And other miniskirted girls in English class
Though none of them had legs like Eleanor's
Perhaps no other girls anywhere
So in order to avert our eyes from Eleanor's legs
We guys kept our eyes riveted on the blackboard
Even when there was no chalk upon it
Even for a few minutes after English class finished

Unfortunately Eleanor had a boyfriend
Who played tight-end on our Senior football team
And caught forward passes from Frank[349]

---

[349] See Chapter 3 "Frank and Suzy."

And stopped forward passes at Eleanor
Because of the enormity of his presence
And our fear of his interceptions
Thus our seeing Eleanor's long legs
Occurred mainly when we were sleeping

As I reflect back warmly on Eleanor
And other girls in high school older than I was
I must admit to my teenager emotions
Feeling more for them than just admiration
And I guess crushes on long-legged older women
Were common among high school boys
Who enjoyed just seeing them and being near them
Trying not to annoy them with our eyes

Afterword

Mr. Perkins[350] and Gwendolyn

For three summers after graduation
Mr. Perkins's baton clicks persisted
When he and his lovely wife Sally
Worked with Marabeth[351] and I at a children's camp
The third summer Sally cared for me kindly
While I resided in her tiny "infirmary"
With a well-earned dose of mononucleosis
Called "the kissing sickness" in those days

An appropriate term in my case
For record-breaking kissing was a nightly occurrence
With the love of my life Gwendolyn
Who insisted on being called "Gwen"
But she was given the camp name "Mrs. America"
Because I was given the camp name "Captain America"[352]

---

[350] See Chapter 4 "Favourite Teacher Mr. Perkins."
[351] Marabeth was the piano accompanist for the Broadway musicals that Mr. Perkins directed (See Chapter 11 "Marabeth the Best of Us").
[352] I had no idea who Captain America was, as I wasn't much into comic books.

And everyone's certain assumption
That one day Gwen and I would marry

Gwen's immune system must have been stronger than mine
Because she kept counselloring on just fine
Even though Gwen had also not slept much
For the previous a month as I can attest
As both of us considered sleeping
To be nothing but a nightly annoyance
To the passion overflowing our hearts
Passion often acted on until dawn

One evening during "Camper Free Time"
When I was "The Watch" walking the rocky shoreline
Watching to make sure no camper fell into the water
I came upon Mr. Perkins and Gwen
In what would have been intense conversation
Except Mr. Perkins was doing all the talking
And Gwen's saddened eyes spoke silently
To what she was hearing but not yet believing

Gwen softly repeated "King's" [353] words to me
Later that evening in disbelief
As we held each other tightly in my sleeping bag
Gwen begging me to relieve her of King's words
Mr. Perkins had told the love of my life
That religion would be an impediment
To any long-term relationship
Especially a relationship that included marriage

Gwen wanted me to firmly declare
No truth in what King had said
Or that his words didn't apply to her

---

[353] Mr. Perkins's camp name was "King."

Or to me or to us and never would
I passionately refuted Mr. Perkins's words
Even after the summer when battered by my father
Who refused to meet the woman I loved
More because of "tradition" [354] than religion

My mother was more sympathetic
And didn't want to lose her eldest over prejudice
And accepted my love for Gwen
And attempted to deflect my father's battering
His shunning of the woman I loved
Caused a schism between my father and me
A schism that would never be sutured
Even after his death at ninety-three

When the fall semester started
Gwen joined me at U of T [355]
From her home in North Ontario [356]
To pursue an "Honours English" degree
We met for lunch daily in Trinity's [357] cafeteria
Across the street from Gwen's St. Hilda's residence
And just an eager 400-metre run
From the Med School that had become a prison

Meeting with Gwen this way was in addition
To my climbing a tree to Gwen's open window

---

[354] The "tradition" of marrying within the Jewish religion is poignantly illustrated in *Fiddler on the Roof* (music by Jerry Bock, lyrics by Sheldon Harnick, and book by Joseph Stein), based on the Sholem Aleichem story, "Tevye and His Daughters." One of Tevye's daughters falls in love with a Christian and is shunned by her father.

[355] University of Toronto.

[356] As I write "North Ontario" in relation to Gwen's home, I am haunted by Neil Young's song "Helpless" that begins with "There's a town in North Ontario" (*Déjà Vu* recorded by Crosby, Stills, Nash & Young in 1970).

[357] Trinity College is the Anglican College at the University of Toronto.

Like Romeo to his Juliet's window
Though I climbed my Juliet's tree more rapidly
For near the top a branch beckoned me
To crawl through Gwen's open window
Like Tony through Maria's in *West Side Story*[358]
To immerse in love's wonder

One evening the matron of St. Hilda's
Caught me climbing through Gwen's window
And gave Gwen a detention instead of me
Even though I told the matron I was a cat burglar[359]
So to be as close to Gwen as possible
I took a room in our quiet Meds frat house[360]
Just a short block from St. Hilda's
And put a DO NOT DISTURB sign on the door

Gwen and I spent every weekend in my room[361]
Except on sparkling autumn afternoons
When Gwen and I took a walk to our favourite make-out spot
Near the abandoned "Don Valley Brickworks"[362]
And we kissed on a quilt of crackling leaves
Of lovely red and gold mosaic patterns

---

[358] *West Side Story* is a Broadway musical brilliantly composed by Leonard Berstein, with lyrics by Stephen Sondheim, choreography by Jerome Robbins, and book by Arthur Laurents. The 1961 film, directed by Robert Wise and Jerome Robbins, won ten Academy Awards including "Best Motion Picture" (https://awardsdatabase.oscars.org/search/results). The more recent film version of *West Side Story* (2021), directed by Steven Spielberg, with screenplay by Tony Kushner, also won many Academy Awards. The more recent film has the advantage of the woman portraying "Maria," Rachel Zegler, doing her own singing, rather than the Marni Nixon "voice-over" she did for Natalie Wood in the first film version (1961).

[359] The matron would have had both of us expelled if she caught my cat burglar witticism.

[360] The antithesis of *Animal House*, directed by John Landis.

[361] The matron assumed Gwen had gone home.

[362] More than a half-century later it is still hard for me to take the DVP from the 401 into downtown Toronto because it goes past the Brickworks.

To the music of songbirds in the trees
Ignoring the cacophony on the DVP[363]

At a frat party[364] I met Gwen's older sister
Whose green eyes were hauntingly similar to Gwen's
But of course not nearly as beautiful
As no eyes could be as beautiful as Gwen's
Gwen's sister was an RN
Who hugged me hard and whispered
"So you're the Jeff I've been hearing so much about"
Then she asked me to dance a slow song with her

Although Gwen had won an academic scholarship
Gwen's passion was dramatic acting
And she achieved the lead in every U of T production
With each glossy program listing her as "Gwendolyn"
The name Gwen told me to never call her
But "Gwendolyn" seemed to add prestige even accomplishment
To just "Gwen" who needed neither
To be the Gwen I adored

By autumn's end we had set a world's record
For the lengthiest love-making that didn't include intercourse
Because Gwen was concerned of the complications of "the pill"
And that condoms didn't ensure perfect protection
Gwen wanted us to continue our alternate measures
Of sexual pleasure and just loving each other
Yet on my birthday Gwen surprised me with
"Jeff it's time to lose my virginity"

But it wasn't pleasurable for either of us
Because Gwen was just giving me her birthday gift

---

[363] Don Valley Parkway.
[364] Our frat parties were subdued compared to the frat party in *Animal House* (1978), directed by John Landis.

A gift Gwen so terribly feared
And my love for her mitigated such future gifts
Not being on "the pill" made pregnancy a real fear
In spite of our meticulous condom precautions
And Gwen was relieved I agreed to her decision
And my love for Gwen just deepened

At year's end Gwen furthered her theatre career
By accepting an acting gig in Australia
And our communication rapidly evaporated
Although I thought about Gwen for years
I eventually married and started a family
And my family made me happy
But I often thought warmly about Gwen
And knew she was better off with someone not committed to
medicine

It was a half-century since I last saw Gwen
When her cousin Scotty our camp's sailing instructor
Called trying to convince me to attend
The camp's "50th Anniversary Reunion"
I told Scotty "I don't go to reunions"
Then sensed his smile come down the phone line
And after a few seconds Scotty effused
"Gwen will be coming to the reunion"

Scotty went on to happily inform me
Gwen was single again like he heard I was
Then burst out laughing "How can you resist coming
When I assure you Gwen will be there"
Scotty knew me well enough to be correct
The possibility of seeing Gwen was an electromagnet
So I took my black jacket to the cleaners
To be pressed to impress Gwen

As I entered the hall of "The 50th"
I was greeted by many "blasts from the past"[365]
But quickly excavated my way through the throng
As my intent was only on finding Gwen
However I couldn't find her but I did find Scotty
And urgently asked him "Where's Gwen"
Scotty put his right hand on my left shoulder
And said "Sorry Jeff Gwen's not coming"

Of course I was more than disappointed
And stood frozen for more than a minute
Then focused on finding Mr. Perkins[366] and Marabeth[367]
As I needed their warmth and affection
But I couldn't find either of them
So I ran to the registration desk
And neither of their names was listed
And as darkness swept over me I left

In the two hour drive back to London
I reflected on what had just happened
And what I could have possibly expected
Yet I couldn't help feeling deflated
I needed to hear Mr. Perkins's baton clicks
And Marabeth's words of consistent friendship
And breathe Gwen's helium in my lungs again
Or drown in the ocean of her absence

---

[365] "Blast from the past" is a pop-radio term for "oldies but goodies."
[366] See Chapter 4 "Favourite Teacher Mr. Perkins."
[367] See Chapter 11 "Marabeth the Best of Us."

Mea Culpa

I'm still alive to write my high school stories
Only because I'm a physician
Who received cancer treatment
Only because I'm a physician
To mitigate a "two years" death sentence
Decreed by the extent of my metastases
And the "bulk" of my "central disease"
Declaring futility of any treatment

But I did receive cancer treatment
Only because I'm a physician
In a teaching hospital of a large medical school
Whose former students broke protocols for me
By inventing cheery possibilities
The degree of my disease was reluctant to concede
And I eagerly agreed to the consent forms
Warning of the complications of radiation and chemotherapy

More important I resigned myself to celebrating
Each day of my time remaining
And the wonderful life I have been given

The best part of which is my children and a special woman
But also persons from my high school years
Who are becoming clearer as I'm nearer my end
For reasons of which I'm not certain
As I peer through nostalgia's gauze curtain

Such as Mr. Perkins[368] who gave me much more
Than teaching me to read a music score
And Mrs. Rose[369] whose Math proposed
I could go straight into Medical School if I chose
And my high school friends who I wish I could be with again
In the snow globe of my limited future
But I know I can't as my closest friend Sam[370]
Can't be with me at my left hand

Yet I'm still here because of Sam
As near his death he insisted I have the PSA test
That I had previously refused because it wasn't publicly funded[371]
And I didn't want to end-run our "universal healthcare" system
And I'm also here because of my children
With whom I discussed "The System's" no-treatment decision
On the sofa of my youngest from which my eldest
Rose to berate me with "Dad you can't accept this"

He insisted I call "Dr. Carey"[372]
An oncologist and close friend
And bass guitarist in our rock band
Who referred me a radiotherapist friend

---

[368] See Chapter 4 "Favourite Teacher Mr. Perkins."
[369] See Chapter 12 "Wild Mrs. Rose."
[370] See Chapter 28 "Gillda and Sam."
[371] The PSA test became publicly funded in most Canadian provinces the year after my diagnosis.
[372] Mark Carey had just returned from a fellowship at MD Anderson Cancer Treatment Center in Houston.

However the radiotherapist thought treatment inappropriate
Saying "We usually don't treat bulky diseases like this
But because you're a physician and Mark's friend
I'll give you radiation but it won't make a difference"

It was easy to respond "Well radiate me then"
But he warned "You'll need chemo in addition"
So I saw a chemotherapist friend I trained with
Whose clinic is just forty paces from my office
He reluctantly agreed to give me chemotherapy
But only after radiation decreased "the bulk" of my disease
So I eagerly trotted down a long hall for radiotherapy
Five days a week to decrease "the bulk" of my disease

For the four months of radiation
I was fortunate complications were few
Then I went on chemo and knew vomiting
 A small price to pay for one more grandchildren-day
And six years later I'm still here
Though well aware cancer will eventually claim me
But also aware I'm privileged to have received treatment
Only because I'm a physician

www.ingramcontent.com/pod-product-compliance
Lightning Source LLC
Chambersburg PA
CBHW030836090426
42737CB00009B/994